# Understanding Research Methods

## An Overview of the Essentials

Mildred L. Patten

Pyrczak Publishing
P.O. Box 39731 • Los Angeles, CA 90039

Project director: Monica Lopez

Editorial assistance provided by Sharon Young, Brenda Koplin, Cheryl Alcorn, and Randall R. Bruce.

Cover design by Robert Kibler and Larry Nichols.

Printed in the United States of America.

ISBN 1-884585-47-7

# CONTENTS

Continued →

# INTRODUCTION

This book provides you with an overview of basic research methods.

**The distinctive features of this book are:**

◆ The division of the material into short sections instead of long chapters will help you take small steps through this exciting but highly technical field of study. The long chapters in other research methods books encourage students to take big gulps, which often are not easily digested.

◆ When one topic builds directly on the previous one, the second one begins with a reminder of what you should have mastered in the first. This helps you keep your eye on the big picture.

◆ Technical jargon is defined in plain English to the extent possible, and numerous examples make abstract research concepts concrete. Student reactions in field tests attest to success in the effort to make this book comprehensible.

◆ The material on statistics is presented at the conceptual level. It shows you how to interpret statistical reports but does not bog you down with computational details.

◆ The exercises at the end of the topics encourage you to pause to make sure you have mastered one topic before moving on to another. This is important because many topics are cumulative—thorough mastery of an earlier one is a prerequisite for mastering a later one with ease. The first part of each exercise tests your comprehension of factual material. The second part asks you to interpret and apply the material you have mastered. This will help you internalize the concepts as well as stimulate classroom discussions.

**Why should you have an overview of research methods? Because . . .**

◆ Leaders in all fields are increasingly relying on the results of research in making important decisions such as how to help those who are dependent on welfare, which types of educational programs to fund, and how to adjust work environments to improve employees' output and satisfaction. If you hope to become a decision-maker in your field, you must master research methods to be effective in sorting through the conflicting claims often found in the research literature on a topic.

◆ Many of you will be expected to do simple but important research on the job. Clinical psychologists are expected to track improvements made by their clients, teachers are expected to experiment with new methods in the classroom, and social workers are expected to collect data on their clients.

◆ All of you will be making lifestyle decisions based on research reported in the media. Should you take vitamin supplements? How should you dress for success on the job? Which make of automobile should you buy if your primary concern is safety? Answers based on research are often offered in newspapers, magazines, and television newscasts. As a result of studying research methods, you will become a sophisticated consumer. You'll consider questions such as "Was the sample biased?" and "Are the results statistically significant?"

◆ Finally, you may need to read and report on published research in other classes. You will be more skilled at doing this if you have an understanding of basic methods of research.

## Acknowledgments

Dr. Anne Hafner and Dr. Robert Morman, both of California State University, Los Angeles, provided many helpful comments on the first draft of this book. Their assistance is greatly appreciated. Errors and omissions, of course, remain the responsibility of the author.

# PART A

## INTRODUCTION TO RESEARCH METHODS

This part of the book defines what we mean by *empirical research* and provides an overview of the characteristics of major approaches to this type of research. Broad issues that underlie all types of research such as the nature of research hypotheses, how researchers define the variables they plan to study, ethical considerations in research, and the relationship between theory and research are also covered in this part.

# NOTES

# TOPIC 1  INTRODUCTION TO EMPIRICAL RESEARCH

The *empirical* approach to knowledge is based on *observations*.[1] We all use the empirical approach in everyday living. For instance, if a teacher observes that students become restless during a certain lesson, he or she might say that they "know" that the lesson is boring. As useful as everyday observations often are, they can be misleading and often are misinterpreted. For example, the teacher may have misinterpreted reasons for the children's restlessness; it might be the time and day, such as a warm Friday afternoon, that is the culprit — not the inherent interest of the lesson. Even if the lesson is boring to this teacher's children, the teacher might conclude that the lesson is boring to children *in general*, when it might, in fact, be interesting to other children at other ability levels, with different backgrounds, and so on.

When scientists use the empirical approach, they strive to avoid misleading results and poor interpretations. The key to doing so is careful planning of *why* they want to make observations, *whom* they wish to observe, as well as *how* and *when* to observe.

The question of *why* to observe establishes the need for the study. Perhaps a better method for helping students acquire a certain mathematics skill is needed. After considering their own experiences and reviewing related literature on the topic, researchers prepare a formal statement of their research purpose such as "whether the use of hands-on manipulatives to teach Topic X will result in greater student achievement than a lecture and workbook approach." They might also arrive at a *hypothesis*, which is a statement of what they expect the results to show. For example, they might hypothesize that those who use manipulatives will have higher scores than those who are exposed to the lecture/workbook approach. The question of *why* is explored throughout Parts A and B of this book.

When they plan *whom* to observe, they first decide whether to observe an entire population

(such as all fifth-grade children in a school district) or just a sample of the population. If a sample is to be observed, which is often the case, they consider how to obtain a sample that is not biased against any individuals or subgroups. For example, asking for students to volunteer to take a lesson might result in a sample of students who are more interested in the content of that lesson than the children in the population as a whole. Such a sample would be biased against those who are less interested in the first place. Methods of drawing unbiased samples are discussed in Part C of this book.

When scientists plan *how* to observe, they select among the available instruments such as objective tests, interviews, and direct observation of behavior, with an eye to selecting the most valid instrument(s). If none is judged to be reasonably valid for their purpose, they develop new instruments. Then, of course, they need to decide *when* they will use the instruments to obtain the most valid results. These issues are explored in detail in Part D of this book.

The observations scientists make may result in *data* in the form of numbers, which are analyzed statistically. Popular statistical techniques are described in Part F of this book. Note that some scientific observations are *not* reduced to numbers but are expressed in words. For example, interview data may be described in a narrative that points out themes and trends. The choice between the two approaches is described in Topics 9 and 10 of this book.

One of the most fundamental distinctions in scientific research is whether research is *experimental* or *nonexperimental*. In experimental research, treatments are given for the research purpose — such as treating some students with manipulatives and others with a lecture/workbook approach in order to determine which treatment *causes* greater achievement.

Of course, we are not always interested in cause-and-effect questions. For example, we

---

[1]Examples of other approaches are (1) *deduction* as when we deduce a proof in mathematics based on certain assumptions and definitions and (2) *reliance on authority* such as relying on a dictator's pronouncements as a source of knowledge.

might want to know whether teachers believe they need more training in the use of manipulatives for teaching mathematics. For this particular purpose, we merely need to ask teachers about their needs; we do not need to train or treat the teachers. The distinction between experimental and nonexperimental research is explored in the next two topics of this book.

# EXERCISE ON TOPIC 1

1. *Observation* is the basis for what approach to knowledge?

2. What does the question of *why* establish?

3. How is the term *hypothesis* defined in this topic?

4. According to the topic, are samples often observed?

5. What do scientists do when they plan *how* to observe?

6. Are the results of all scientific studies expressed as numbers?

7. Are treatments given for the research purpose in *experimental* or *nonexperimental* research?

## Questions for Discussion

8. Briefly describe a time when you were misled by everyday observation, that is, when you reached a conclusion based on everyday observation that you later decided was an incorrect conclusion.

9. You have probably encountered conflicting research reported in the mass media. For example, one study might indicate that X increases blood pressure while another study indicates that X does not increase it. Speculate on the reasons why different researchers might obtain different results when studying the same problem.

## For Students Who Are Planning Research

10. Name a general problem area in which you might conduct research. At this point, your problem area may still be broad such as "HIV education" or it may be narrow such as "effectivness of the Jones' HIV education program for high school juniors." Also, you may wish to name several problem areas for research and make a final selection at a later time.

11. Have you already made observations in your problem area(s)? If so, briefly describe them. (Keep in mind that observations may be *direct* such as observing aggressive behavior on a playground or *indirect* such as asking adolescents for self-reports on their alcohol consumption.)

12. If you answered yes to question 11, did you make informal observations *or* did you plan *why*, *whom*, and *how* to observe in advance of making the observations? Explain.

# TOPIC 2  EXPERIMENTAL VS. NONEXPERIMENTAL STUDIES

In **experiments**, researchers give treatments and observe to see if they cause changes in behavior. A classic simple experiment is one in which we form two groups at random and give each group a different treatment. To form two groups at random, we can put the names of the available subjects on slips of paper, mix them thoroughly and pull some names for each group.[1] Notice that random assignment gives each subject an equal chance of being in either group.

Here are two examples of experiments:

EXAMPLE 1
Fifty students were divided into two groups at random. One group received math instruction via a correspondence course on the Internet. The other group was given instruction on the same math skills using a traditional textbook and workbook approach. The purpose was to see if instruction via the Internet was more effective than traditional instruction.

In Example 1, the group receiving the new type of instruction via the Internet is referred to as the *experimental group* while the group receiving traditional instruction is called the *control group*.

When the subjects are divided at random (such as drawing names out of a hat to determine who will be in the experimental and who will be in the control group), the experiment is called a *true experiment*. Not all experiments are true experiments,[2] as illustrated by Example 2.

EXAMPLE 2
A psychiatrist identified 100 clinically depressed clients who volunteered to take a new drug under her direction. She identified an additional 100 nonvolunteers with the same diagnosis and similar demographics (that is, background characteristics such as age and gender) to serve as controls. The study was conducted to investigate the effectiveness of the new drug in treating depression.

In Example 2, the experiment was conducted by comparing the volunteers who were given the new drug with the nonvolunteers. This study is an experiment even though random assignment was not used. Note that if a researcher administers treatments or arranges for their administration, the study is called an experiment whether or not groups of subjects are formed at random.

In **nonexperimental studies**, researchers do *not* give treatments. Rather, they observe subjects in order to describe them as they naturally exist without experimental intervention. One of the most common types of nonexperimental studies is the *survey* or poll in which subjects are interviewed, questioned, or otherwise observed in order to determine their attitudes, beliefs, and behavior as they exist without experimental intervention.

Nonexperimental studies come in many forms, which are explored in more detail in Topic 4. At this point, however, you should be able to distinguish between nonexperimental studies and experiments by determining whether treatments were administered for experimental purposes.

Note that you cannot distinguish between nonexperimental and experimental studies on the basis of the type of instrument (that is, measuring tool) used. Instruments such as paper-and-pencil tests, interview schedules, and personality scales are used in both types of studies. The act of measurement is usually not considered to be a treatment. In fact, researchers try to measure in such a way that the act of measuring does *not* affect or change the subjects. This is true in both experimental and nonexperimental studies.

By now, you may have inferred that the purpose of an experiment is to explore cause-and-effect relationships (that is, treatments are given to see how they affect the subjects). In the next topic, you will learn how nonexperimental studies also are sometimes used for this purpose.

---

[1]Other methods for drawing random samples are discussed in Part C of this book.
[2]Types of experiments are explored more fully in Part E, where you will learn the advantages of true experiments.

# EXERCISE ON TOPIC 2

1. In which type of study are treatments given?

2. In an experiment, Group A was given verbal praise for being on time for appointments while Group B was given no special treatment. Which group is the control group?

3. When subjects are divided at random, what type of experiment is being conducted?

4. What is the purpose of a nonexperimental study?

5. Is a survey an experiment?

6. Does knowing that interviews were used in a study help you determine whether the study was experimental or nonexperimental?

7. What is the major purpose of an experiment?

8. A social worker surveyed clients to determine their satisfaction with the services provided. Is this an experimental study or nonexperimental study?

9. A teacher tried three methods of teaching handwriting by using different methods with different students. Is this an experimental study or nonexperimental study?

## Questions for Discussion

10. Suppose you read that an outbreak of intestinal disorders occurred in a town and the source was traced to contaminated chicken served in a popular restaurant. Is it likely that the study that identified the source was experimental or nonexperimental? Why?

11. Have you ever conducted an informal experiment by giving a treatment to a person or a group and observing the effects? If so, briefly describe it. Would you have obtained better information by including a control group? Explain.

12. Suppose you wanted to know whether reading to preschool children has a positive effect on subsequent reading achievement. Do you think that it would be better to conduct an experimental or a nonexperimental study? Why?

## For Students Who Are Planning Research

13. At this point, do you anticipate using an experimental or nonexperimental approach in your research? If it will be experimental, what treatments do you plan to administer?

# TOPIC 3  EXPERIMENTAL VS. CAUSAL-COMPARATIVE STUDIES

As you know from Topic 2, an **experiment** is a study in which treatments are given in order to observe their effects. When we conduct experiments, we ask, "Do the treatments (i.e., the input or stimulus) *cause* changes in the subjects' behavior (i.e., the output or response)?"

When we want to investigate cause-and-effect relationships, we usually prefer experimental over nonexperimental studies. However, there are times when cause-and-effect is of concern, but conducting an experiment is not possible for physical, ethical, legal, or financial reasons. An example is the effects of smoking on health. It would be unethical (because of potential harm to the subjects) to treat some subjects with smoke (such as requiring them to smoke a pack of cigarettes a day for 15 years) in order to observe the effects in comparison with a nonsmoking control group (which is forbidden to smoke for 15 years). Clearly, for this research problem, we cannot conduct an experiment. Notice that even if it were ethical to conduct such an experiment, it may not be practical because we probably would not want to wait 15 years to determine the answer to such an important question.

When it is impossible or impractical to conduct an experiment on a question of causality, we must settle for information derived from nonexperimental studies. For example, we can identify both people who currently have lung cancer and a control group with similar demographics (that is, background characteristics such as socioeconomic status) and describe the differences between the two groups in terms of previous lifestyle characteristics that might affect health such as diet, exercise, smoking, prescription drug use, illicit substance abuse, and so on. A finding that smoking differentiates between the two groups while other lifestyle characteristics do not *points the finger* at smoking as a possible cause of lung cancer.

However, there are several dangers in this interpretation. First, smoking and cancer might

have a common cause. For example, perhaps stress causes cancer, and stress also causes people to smoke excessively. If this is the case, banning smoking will not prevent cancer; only reducing stress will. Another danger is that the researcher may have failed to identify control subjects who were properly matched with those who have lung cancer. For instance, perhaps most of those with lung cancer reside in urban areas and those in the control group tend to reside in rural areas. Since urban areas tend to have more smog than rural areas, smog might be the cause, and smoking might be coincidental. These types of problems would not arise in a true experiment in which subjects are divided at random to form two groups— one of which will be made to smoke and the other forbidden to smoke. They would not be problems because the random assignment would produce two groups that are equally likely to experience stress and equally likely to live in either rural or urban areas—and, in fact, be about equal[1] in terms of all other potential causes of cancer.[2]

The example of smoking and lung cancer illustrates a specific type of nonexperimental study known as a **causal-comparative study** (sometimes called an *ex post facto study*).[3] The essential characteristics of this type of nonexperimental study are that (1) we observe and describe some current condition (such as lung cancer) and (2) we look to the past to try to identify the possible cause(s) of the condition. Notice that researchers do *not* give any treatments in causal-comparative studies. They only describe observations; hence, they are conducting nonexperimental studies. Although the causal-comparative method has more potential pitfalls than the experimental method, it is often the best we can do when attempting to explore causality. However, when it is used properly, the causal-comparative method is a powerful scientific tool that provides data for many important decisions that are made in all the sciences.

---

[1]The larger the sample, the more likely they will be equal. Sample size is covered in Topics 21 and 22.
[2]The relationship between smoking and health has been examined in hundreds of causal-comparative studies. Most experts agree that alternative interpretations are without merit.
[3]Other types of nonexperimental studies are covered in the next topic.

# EXERCISE ON TOPIC 3

1. According to the topic, do experimental *or* causal-comparative studies have more potential pitfalls when trying to identify cause-and-effect relationships?

2. We look to the past for a cause in which type of study?

3. Is causal-comparative research a type of experiment?

4. What is another name for a causal-comparative study?

5. Are treatments given by researchers in causal-comparative studies?

6. Random assignment to treatments is used in which type of study?

7. A researcher compared the health of adolescents who had received free lunches during their elementary school years with that of a comparable group of children who had not received free lunches. The purpose was to determine the effects of free lunch on health. Did the researcher conduct an experimental or causal-comparative study?

8. A researcher divided patients who were being released from the hospital into two groups. One group received the normal exit interview and counseling while another was given an extended exit interview and extended counseling. The purpose was to determine the effects of the two types of interviews and counseling on patients' compliance with physicians' orders during the first week after hospitalization. Did the researcher conduct an experimental or a causal-comparative study?

9. Suppose a researcher wants to know the effects of smog on lung cancer rates. Will a causal-comparative or experimental study provide an answer in a shorter amount of time?

## Questions for Discussion

10. If you wanted to investigate the causes of child abuse, would you probably use the experimental or causal-comparative method? Why?

11. Suppose you read that a causal-comparative study indicates that those who take vitamins A and E tend to be less overweight than the general population. Are there any possible dangers in the interpretation that the vitamins *cause* people to maintain a healthy weight?

## For Students Who Are Planning Research

12. If you will be conducting a nonexperimental study, will it be causal-comparative (i.e., will you be looking to the past for the causes of some current condition)? If yes, briefly explain why you chose this method of research instead of the experimental method.

# TOPIC 4 TYPES OF NONEXPERIMENTAL RESEARCH

As you know from Topics 2 and 3, researchers do not give treatments to subjects in nonexperimental studies. Rather, they observe (that is, measure) in order to describe the subjects without trying to change them.

Nonexperimental studies take many forms because they serve many purposes. Some of the more common types of nonexperimental studies and their purposes are described here.

You learned in the previous topic about **causal-comparative research** in which we look to the past for the cause(s) of a current condition.

Another type you are already familiar with is the **survey** or *poll*. The purpose of surveys is to describe the attitudes, beliefs, and behavior of a population. We draw a sample of a population, study the sample and then make inferences to the population from the sample data. For example, we could survey a sample of all people receiving food stamps to determine what types of food they purchase with the stamps. What we learn from this sample, we can generalize to the population, assuming that we have drawn a good sample.[1] Note that if we decide not to sample but, instead, interview everyone in the population (that is, all people receiving food stamps), the study would be called a **census**. A census is a count or study of all members of a population.

While surveys usually include hundreds or thousands of subjects, a **case study** usually involves only one. For instance, many important theories in clinical psychology were developed based on intensive one-on-one case studies of individuals. In a case study, the emphasis is on obtaining thorough knowledge of an individual — sometimes over a long period of time. We do not confine ourselves to asking a limited number of questions on a one-shot basis as we usually do in surveys.

When we conduct a thorough, intensive case study of a group—such as a tribe or all people affiliated with a public school—we usually say that we are conducting **field research** (also called *ethnographic research*).[2] When conducting this type of research, we might observe as an outsider, or we might become a member of the group in order to make the observations. For example, a nurse researcher might join the staff of a hospital as an employee in order to conduct his or her field research on the hospital.

When we repeatedly measure trait(s) of the subjects over a period of time in order to trace developmental trends, we say that we are conducting **longitudinal research**. For example, we could measure the visual acuity of a sample of infants each week for a year to trace its development.

In **correlational research**, we are interested in the degree of relationship among two or more quantitative *variables*. For example, scores on a college admissions test and GPAs are quantitative and, because people *vary* or differ on both of them, they are variables.[3] If we conduct a study in which we are asking "Did those with high admissions scores tend to earn high GPAs?" and "Did those with low admissions scores tend to earn low GPAs?" we are asking a correlational question. If the answer is "yes," we can say that the test works (i.e., is valid for predicting GPAs).[4]

Finally, in **historical research**, we examine data in order to understand the past. Note that good historical research is not just a matter of developing a chronological list of so-called facts and dates. Rather, it is an attempt to understand the dynamics of human history. As such, it is driven by theories and hypotheses, just like other types of research. In other words, by reviewing historical evidence, researchers are able to develop theories that may explain historical events and patterns. These theories lead to hypotheses, which are evaluated in terms of additional historical data that are collected.

---

[1] Characteristics of good samples are explored in detail in Part C of this book.
[2] Ethnographic research is a type of qualitative research, which is discussed in more detail in Topics 9 and 10.
[3] Types of variables are described in Topics 5 and 6.
[4] Validity is explored in Part D. Correlational studies employ a statistic called a *correlation coefficient*, which is described in Topic 47.

# EXERCISE ON TOPIC 4

1. Suppose a researcher annually administered an intelligence test to young children to study changes in intelligence over time. She was conducting what type of study?

2. Is the study in question 1 experimental?

3. If a researcher conducts a poll to estimate public support for free child care for welfare mothers, he is conducting what type of nonexperimental study?

4. An investigator determined the degree of relationship between vocabulary scores and reading comprehension scores. She was conducting what type of nonexperimental study?

5. What is another name for field research?

6. A case study usually involves how many subjects?

## Questions for Discussion

7. Name a topic in your field of study that you might explore with a nonexperimental study. Which type of study would be most appropriate for your topic?

8. Think of a survey in which you were asked to serve as a subject. (You may have been sent a questionnaire in the mail such as a consumer satisfaction survey or been contacted in person or by phone.) Did you cooperate and respond? Why? Why not?

9. Name two quantitative variables that might be studied using correlational research.

10. Suppose someone prepared a list of educational events and their dates of occurrence in this century. Would the list be an example of "good" historical research? Explain.

## For Students Who Are Planning Research

11. If you will be conducting a nonexperimental study, which type will it be? Explain the basis for your choice.

# TOPIC 5  VARIABLES IN NONEXPERIMENTAL STUDIES

A **variable** is a trait or characteristic with two or more categories. Subjects *vary* in terms of the categories. Here's an example:

EXAMPLE 1
A sample of registered voters was surveyed. Each was asked to name his or her gender (male or female) and the candidate for whom he or she planned to vote (Doe, Jones, or Smith). The purpose was to explore gender differences in voting preferences.

In Example 1, there are two variables: (1) the preferred candidate — with three categories and (2) gender—with two categories.

Be careful not to confuse a variable with its categories. For instance, "male" is one of the two *categories* of the *variable* called "gender"; "male" is *not* a variable. Here's how to visualize it:

One variable $\Longrightarrow$ *GENDER*

Two categories $\Longrightarrow$ | Male | Female |

All variables have *mutually exclusive* categories. That is, each subject will belong to one and only one category. For instance, the categories for "preferred candidate" are mutually exclusive because we ask, "For which *one* candidate do you plan to vote?" When conducting such a survey, we would not allow a subject to name two candidates (that is, two categories) for the same political office.

We also try to define variables in such a way that the categories are *exhaustive*. For instance, if there are only three candidates on the ballot, but voters are also allowed to write in the names of additional candidates, we should define the preferred candidate variable as having these categories: Doe, Jones, Smith, and Other. The "Other" category makes the list of categories all inclusive —or exhaustive.

Notice that both variables in Example 1 are "naming" variables (more properly called "categorical" variables).[1] Each subject "names" his or her gender and the preferred candidate. Other variables have quantitative categories that measure the amount of a characteristic. Consider Example 2.

EXAMPLE 2
The college admissions scores on the *Scholastic Aptitude Test* (*SAT*) were compared with students' freshman GPAs to determine how valid the *SAT* is for predicting GPAs.

Both *SAT* scores (ranging from 200 to 800 per subtest) and GPAs (usually ranging from 0.00 to 4.00) are quantitative. In other words, the quantities are the categories. A student who earns an *SAT* score of 550 belongs to the category called "550."

Variables in nonexperimental studies are sometimes classified as being either *independent* or *dependent*. For example, when we conduct a causal-comparative study (see Topic 3 to review) the presumed cause is called the *independent* variable and the effect is called the *dependent* variable. Remember:

| The *independent* (stimulus or input) variable causes changes in the *dependent* (response or output) variable. |

Some researchers refer to any variable that comes first (whether or not it is presumed to be a cause) as "independent" and to the one that comes later as "dependent." For instance, usually *SAT* scores (the predictor variable) are determined before students earn their GPAs. Thus, some would call the *SAT* the independent variable and the GPA the dependent variable.[2]

The terms *independent* and *dependent variable* are explored more fully in Topic 6.

---

[1]*Naming data* are obtained from the *nominal scale of measurement*. Scales of measurement are discussed in Topic 39.
[2]It is also common to call the predictor variable the *predictor* and the outcome variable the *criterion*.

# EXERCISE ON TOPIC 5

1. Adults who were taking a course to learn English as a second language were asked to name their country of birth and their number of years of formal education. In this example, how many variables were being studied?

2. In question 1, which variable is a categorical variable?

3. In question 1, which variable is quantitative?

4. A sample of adults was asked their level of agreement with the statement, "The President of the United States is doing a good job in foreign relations." They were permitted to respond either "strongly agree," "agree," "disagree," or "strongly disagree." How many variables were being studied?

5. What is meant by *mutually exclusive categories*?

6. A researcher looked for the causes of social unrest by examining economic variables such as poverty, income, and so on. Is social unrest an independent or dependent variable?

7. If we administer a basic math test before students take algebra to see if it predicts achievement in high school algebra as measured by an algebra test given at the end of Algebra I, what is the dependent variable?

8. If we ask subjects to state their age as being in one of these categories: "under 21," "21-39," "40-55," and "56+," are we using exhaustive categories?

9. In question 8, how many variables are being studied?

10. What is the minimum number of categories on a variable?

## Questions for Discussion

11. Suppose you want to measure income on a self-report questionnaire in which subjects will check off their income category. Name the categories you would use. Are they exhaustive and mutually exclusive? Explain.

12. Name a quantitative variable of interest to you and name its categories. Are the categories mutually exclusive and exhaustive? Explain.

## For Students Who Are Planning Research

13. If you will be conducting a nonexperimental study, name the major variables you will be studying. For each, indicate whether or not the categories will be quantitative.

# Topic 6  Variables in Experimental Studies

All experiments have at least one **independent variable** and one **dependent variable**. The purpose of experiments is to estimate the extent to which independent variables cause changes in dependent variables.

As you know from the previous section, an independent variable is a stimulus or input variable. Note that in experiments, researchers *physically manipulate* independent variables. By "physically manipulate," we mean that the researcher does something physical to the subjects. Examples of physical manipulation are (1) giving a new drug to some subjects while giving a placebo to others and (2) providing some students with computers while denying computers to others. Thus, to *physically manipulate* means to physically administer treatments.

Note that in nonexperimental studies, researchers do *not* physically manipulate independent variables. Instead, they observe independent variables as they occur (or have occurred) naturally. For example, we observe the health of people who have smoked cigarettes in nonexperimental studies—we do not provide subjects with cigarettes nor do we expose them to smoke. (See Topic 3 to review other differences between experimental and nonexperimental studies of causation.)

In a simple experiment, there is one independent variable and one dependent variable, as in Example 1.

EXAMPLE 1
A disruptive student is given extra praise every other week for being in his seat when appropriate. The purpose of the study is to see if the extra praise will increase the amount of appropriate in-seat behavior.

In Example 1, the physical manipulation is giving or not giving extra praise, which is the independent variable. The dependent variable is changes in the student's in-seat behavior.

Often experiments have more than one dependent variable. For instance, in Example 1, we could observe not only to see if the treatment causes more in-seat behavior but also to see if the student's achievement increases and if his attitude toward school improves. If we did so, we would have three dependent variables.

Many experiments also have more than one independent variable. Often, these are more interesting than those with one independent variable because they give us greater insight into causality. Consider Example 2.

EXAMPLE 2
Voluntary, free job training was offered to all welfare mothers in a small city. Four groups of the mothers were formed at random to explore the effects of these two independent variables: (1) providing or not providing free child care while in training and (2) providing or not providing transportation money to get to the job-training site. Each group was assigned at random to one of the four treatment conditions shown here:

| GROUP 1<br>child care<br>*and*<br>transportation money | GROUP 3<br>*no* child care<br>*and*<br>transportation money |
|---|---|
| GROUP 2<br>child care<br>*and*<br>*no* transportation<br>money | GROUP 4<br>*no* child care<br>*and*<br>*no* transportation<br>money |

It was predicted that those in Group 1 would have the highest participation rates, those in Group 2 would have the next highest, those in Group 3 would have the next highest, and those in Group 4 would have the lowest.

Notice that in Example 2 we can determine (1) how effective child care is, (2) how effective transportation money is, and (3) how effective both child care *and* transportation money *in combination* are. Thus, we get more information by looking at two independent variables in one study than by looking at each independent variable in a separate experiment (in which case, we could determine only points 1 and 2).

# Exercise on Topic 6

1. All experiments have at least how many dependent variables?

2. In an experiment, which variable is the stimulus or input variable?

3. What does *physically manipulate* mean in an experimental context?

4. Are dependent variables physically manipulated?

5. Can an experiment have more than one independent variable?

6. Every other customer entering a shoe store was given a different coupon. One offered a second pair of shoes for 50% off. The other offered to reduce the total price by 25% if two pairs of shoes were purchased. The purpose was to determine which coupon was more effective in getting people to buy two pairs of shoes. In this experiment, what is the independent variable?

7. In question 6, what is the dependent variable?

8. A teacher showed an AIDS education film to one group of students and gave a handout on the same material to another group. The purpose was to determine which was more effective in increasing students' knowledge of AIDS prevention. In this experiment, what is the dependent variable?

9. In question 8, what is the independent variable?

## Questions for Discussion

10. Name a variable that would be easy for you to physically manipulate in an experiment. Then, name a variable that might be affected by your manipulation.

11. Name a variable that you could or would not be willing to physically manipulate for ethical or legal reasons.

## For Students Who Are Planning Research

12. If you will be conducting an experiment, name the independent and dependent variables you will be studying.

# TOPIC 7 RESEARCH HYPOTHESES, PURPOSES, AND QUESTIONS

A **research hypothesis** is a prediction of the outcome of a study. The prediction may be based on an educated guess or a formal theory. Example 1 is a hypothesis for a nonexperimental study.

EXAMPLE 1
It is hypothesized that first-grade girls will show better reading comprehension than first-grade boys.

In Example 1, the author is predicting that he or she will find higher comprehension among girls than boys. To test it, a nonexperimental study would be appropriate because nothing in the hypothesis suggests that treatments will be given.

A simple research hypothesis predicts a relationship between two variables. From your study of variables in the previous sections, it should be clear that the two variables in Example 1 are (1) gender and (2) reading comprehension. The hypothesis states that reading comprehension is related to gender.

Example 2 is a hypothesis for an experimental study.

EXAMPLE 2
It is hypothesized that children who are shown a video with mild violence will be more aggressive on the playground than those who are shown a similar video without the violence.

In Example 2, the *independent variable* is violence (mild vs. none), and the *dependent variable* is aggressiveness on the playground.

The hypotheses in Examples 1 and 2 are examples of **directional hypotheses**. In a directional hypothesis, we predict which group will be higher or have more of something.

Sometimes we have a **nondirectional** hypothesis. Consider Example 3.

EXAMPLE 3
It is hypothesized that the child-rearing practices of Tribe A are different from those of Tribe B.

The author of Example 3 is saying that there will be a difference but does not predict the direction of the difference. This is perfectly acceptable when there is no basis for making an educated guess.

Instead of a nondirectional hypothesis, we might state a **research purpose**. Example 4 shows a research purpose that corresponds to the nondirectional hypothesis in Example 3.

EXAMPLE 4
The purpose is to explore the differences in child-rearing practices between Tribe A and Tribe B.

A **research question** may also be substituted for a nondirectional hypothesis. Example 5 shows a research question that corresponds to the non-directional hypothesis in Example 3.

EXAMPLE 5
The research question is, "How do the child-rearing practices in Tribe A and Tribe B differ?"

When using a research question as the basis for research, we usually should be careful *not* to state it as a question that can be answered with a simple "yes" or "no," as is done in Example 6.

EXAMPLE 6
The question is, "Do the child-rearing practices in Tribe A and Tribe B differ?"

Example 6 merely ask,s "Do they differ?" This is not a very interesting research question. Example 5 is superior because it asks "*How* do they differ?"

The choice between a nondirectional hypothesis, a research purpose, and a research question is purely a matter of personal taste—all are acceptable in the scientific community. Of course, when we are willing to predict the outcome of a study, we should state a directional hypothesis— not a research purpose or question.

If you've read research reports, you may have encountered references to another type of hypothesis—the **null hypothesis**. This is a *statistical hypothesis*, which will be explored in Part F of this book.

# EXERCISE ON TOPIC 7

1. Which type of statement (hypothesis, purpose, or question) predicts the outcome of a study?

2. "It is hypothesized that college students who have firm career goals achieve higher GPAs than those who do not have firm career goals." Is this a directional or nondirectional hypothesis?

3. Would an experimental or nonexperimental study be better for testing the hypothesis in question 2?

4. "It is hypothesized that children of immigrants and children of native-born citizens will differ in their attitudes toward school." Is this a directional or nondirectional hypothesis?

5. "The goal of this study is to examine college students' attitudes toward religion." Is this statement a hypothesis or purpose?

6. "Are children of alcoholics different from children of nonalcoholics in their social adjustment?" Is this research question stated appropriately? Why? Why not?

7. When we are willing to predict the outcome of a study, should we state a directional or nondirectional hypothesis?

8. What are the two alternatives to stating a nondirectional hypothesis?

## Questions for Discussion

9. Restate this hypothesis as a research purpose: "It is hypothesized that there is a difference in job satisfaction between those who receive regular feedback on their job performance and those who receive irregular feedback."

10. Is the hypothesis in question 9 directional or nondirectional? Explain.

11. Could an experiment be conducted to test the hypothesis in question 9? Explain.

12. Restate this hypothesis as a research question: "It is hypothesized that those who exercise regularly and those who do not exercise regularly will differ in other behaviors that affect health."

## For Students Who Are Planning Research

13. State a research hypothesis, purpose, or question for your research. (Note: You may have more than one of each.)

14. If you stated a hypothesis in response to question 13, is it directional or nondirectional?

# TOPIC 8  OPERATIONAL DEFINITIONS OF VARIABLES

Dictionaries provide us with **conceptual definitions** of variables. For example, in research on speech communication, we might be interested in students' ability to *recite*, which is defined in one dictionary as "to repeat or speak aloud from or as from memory, especially in a formal way." This definition is perfectly adequate if we merely want to communicate the general topic of our research to someone.

Let's suppose that we want to conduct an experiment on the effectiveness of two memory aids on the ability to recite. As we plan the research, we will soon realize that a conceptual definition is not adequate because it does not indicate the precise concrete or physical steps we will take in order to see the variable. Redefining a variable in terms of physical steps is called *operationalizing* a variable. When we operationalize a variable, we are creating an **operational definition**. Example 1 shows the first attempt at creating an operational definition of students' ability to recite:

EXAMPLE 1
The ability to recite is defined as the number of words mispronounced, missing, or misplaced when students repeat Christian Abzab's poem, *The Road Taken*, aloud from memory in front of a panel of three teachers.

Example 1 is not bad for a first attempt. However, notice that it is not fully operational because we might still ask questions about the physical arrangement such as, "Will the students stand while reciting?," "In what type of room will the recitation take place — a classroom or auditorium?," "Will the teachers be male or female?," and "Will the teachers already know the students?"

It is important to note that operationalizing is a matter of degree. No operational definition is completely operational because there are an infinite number of physical characteristics that might be considered (for example, the humidity in the room, the level of lighting, the type of flooring,

the color of the walls). Thus, instead of striving for completely operational definitions, we try to produce definitions that are adequate to permit a *replication* in all important respects by another researcher. A replication is an attempt to confirm the results of a study by conducting it again in the same way.[1] Of course, there is some subjectivity in applying this criterion of adequacy, and we may not all agree on when we have met it.

Notice that just because a definition is operational does not necessarily mean that it is meaningful or relevant. For example, we could operationalize clients' self-esteem with the definition in Example 2.

EXAMPLE 2
Positive self-esteem is defined as answering "yes" when asked the question, "Do you feel good about yourself?"

The definition in Example 2 is reasonably operational because we know what words to say and what response to listen for. However, it is quite narrow. For example, it does not tap self-esteem in the various dimensions of clients' lives such as self-esteem in the workplace, in social settings, and so on. Thus, a definition can be operational without being adequate in other respects.

Notice that if a researcher fails to provide operational definitions of variables, the definitions still exist since the researcher has to go through physical steps to conduct the research. That is, the definitions exist but may be unstated. When they are unstated, it is difficult, if not impossible, to replicate the research. Thus, providing operational definitions is an important activity when conducting research.

---

[1]Results that have been replicated by independent researchers are those in which we have the most confidence because a given researcher may have blind spots, unconscious biases, etc. Also, a given researcher may have been unlucky and have large random errors in his or her results. Independent replications by others reduce the odds that these factors are the cause of a certain type of result.

# EXERCISE ON TOPIC 8

1. Which type of definition indicates physical steps?

2. In practice, are operational definitions ever fully operationalized?

3. Which of the following definitions of *gregarious* is more operational?
   A. Talking on the phone with friends for at least two hours each week.
   B. Being open and friendly when in social gatherings with others.

4. Which of the following definitions of being *computer literate* is more operational?
   A. Taking at least two formal courses of instruction on the use of computers in an accredited school.
   B. Having knowledge of the origins and uses of computers in modern society and their implications.

5. To replicate the research of others, do we need operational or conceptual definitions?

6. Is it possible for an operational definition to be too narrow?

## Questions for Discussion

7. Suppose you read a research report claiming that low socioeconomic (SES) children have lower self-concepts than high SES children. In the report, the only definition of self-concept is "feeling good about oneself." How much credence would you give the results in light of the definition? What additional information, if any, would you want about the definition if you were planning to replicate the study?

8. In a research report, job satisfaction is defined as "the number of times each subject said 'yes' to questions such as 'Do you look forward to going to work on most mornings?'" Is this definition completely operational? If not, what is missing from the definition?

9. Is the definition in question 8 too narrow in terms of how we normally think about job satisfaction?

10. Write a definition of "success in college" that is highly operational.

11. Write a definition of "motivation to succeed on the job" that is highly operational.

## For Students Who Are Planning Research

12. Name the major variables you will be studying. Define each, trying to be as operational as possible. (Note: After you have read published research on your topic, you may wish to come back here and re-define some of your variables in light of how other researchers have defined them.)

# Topic 9  Quantitative vs. Qualitative Research: I

As you can probably guess, **quantitative research** is research in which the results are presented as quantities or numbers (that is, statistics) and **qualitative research** is research in which the results are trends or themes that are described in words. However, this is an oversimplification since there are many features that distinguish the two types. To understand some of the major differences, let's consider an example.

Suppose a metropolitan police force is demoralized — with signs such as high rates of absenteeism, failure to follow procedures, and so on. Furthermore, the press has raised questions about the effectiveness of the force and its leadership. In such a situation, the police commission might call in a researcher who is assigned the task of identifying possible causes and solutions.

If a quantitative researcher is retained, she would probably begin with a review of the research literature on demoralized police departments. From the review, she would attempt to develop hypotheses to be explored in her research. This is a *deductive approach* to planning the research, that is, she is deducing from the literature possible explanations (that is, hypotheses) to be tested in the research. In contrast, a qualitative researcher would tend to use an *inductive approach* to planning the research. He might, for example, begin to gather data on the specific police force in question and use the very early, preliminary findings as a basis for planning other research activities. In fact, *some* qualitative researchers consciously avoid considering previous research since it might color the way they look at a given situation.

When deciding what types of instruments (that is, measuring tools) to use, a quantitative researcher would tend to emphasize those that produce data that can quickly be reduced to numbers such as structured questionnaires or interview schedules with objective formats such as multiple choice questions. In contrast, a qualitative researcher would tend to emphasize instruments that yield words such as unstructured interviews or direct, unstructured observations of police force officers and their administrators.

When deciding which members of the force to use as subjects, a quantitative researcher would tend to select a large sample, which is made possible within a limited research budget by objective instruments such as an anonymous, objective questionnaire that takes little time to administer.[1] A qualitative researcher will tend to select a small sample for the reverse reason.

When conducting the research, a quantitative researcher would tend to spend a small amount of time directly interacting with the subjects (largely because the nature of her instruments do not require it). A qualitative researcher, on the other hand, might spend a considerable amount of time interviewing and observing various members of the force over an extended period.

While working with the subjects,[2] a qualitative researcher would be open to the possibility of making adjustments in the instruments such as reformulating questions or adding questions based on earlier responses by subjects. A quantitative researcher would seldom make such adjustments.

Also, a quantitative researcher would tend to summarize all responses with statistics and seldom report on individual subjects. A qualitative researcher would tend to cite individuals' responses (such as quoting individual subjects) in the results section of a report.

Finally, a quantitative researcher would tend to generalize her results to one or more populations, while a qualitative researcher would tend to limit his conclusions to individuals who were directly studied.

Should the police commission select a quantitative or qualitative researcher? Criteria for making such a decision are described in the next topic.

---

[1]In addition, she will usually attempt to select a *random sample* in which all subjects have an equal chance of being selected; this can be done, for example, by drawing names out of a hat. The uses of random samples and their relationship to statistics are discussed in later topics. A qualitative researcher is more likely to select a *purposive* sample of people she believes are key in terms of social dynamics, leadership, etc.

[2]Note that quantitative researchers tend to use the terms "subjects" or "respondents" whereas qualitative researchers tend to use the term "participants."

# EXERCISE ON TOPIC 9

1. Do qualitative or quantitative researchers tend to rely more on literature in planning research?

2. Which method of research relies on the inductive approach?

3. Which method of research is more likely to lead to a statistical report of results?

4. In which method of research would a researcher be more likely to modify, add, and delete interview questions during the course of a research project?

5. In which method of research is the interaction between the researcher and the subjects more intense and lengthy?

6. There are more likely to be quotations from subjects in the results sections of reports on which type of research?

7. In which type of research is the investigator less interested in generalizing the results to a population?

## Questions for Discussion

8. In general, are you more likely to believe research results that are presented as themes and trends expressed in words or results described with statistics? Explain. (If you have not read academic research extensively, consider secondary reports of research such as those found in newspapers, magazines, and textbooks.)

9. Do you believe that both qualitative and quantitative research have valuable roles in advancing knowledge in your field of study? Why? Why not?

## For Students Who Are Planning Research

10. At this point, are you leaning toward conducting qualitative or quantitative research? Explain the basis for your choice. (Note that you will be learning more about qualitative research in the next topic.)

In the last topic, we finished with the question, "Should the police commission select a quantitative or qualitative researcher?" Some of the criteria that should be considered when making such a decision are:

A. Some research questions inherently lend themselves more to the quantitative or qualitative approach. For example, "What is the impact of AIDS on the U.S. economy?" is a question that lends itself to quantitative research since the economy is usually measured with numbers. On the other hand, "What is the emotional impact of AIDS on at-risk health care workers?" is a question that lends itself more to the qualitative approach than the first question since it focuses on emotional impact—although it could be examined with either qualitative or quantitative research depending on the orientation of the researcher.

B. When little is known about a topic, qualitative research usually should be initially favored. New topics are constantly emerging in all fields: new diseases such as HIV, new crimes such as car-jacking, and new educational techniques such as putting students on the Internet. On new topics, there will be very little, if any, research literature and, perhaps, no theory with direct applications. In their absence, quantitative researchers may find it difficult to employ the deductive approach. Also, quantitative researchers might find it difficult to write structured questions about a little-known topic. How can you know exactly what to ask when you know little about a topic? In contrast, a qualitative researcher could start with broad questions and refine them during the course of the interviews as various themes and issues start to emerge. Based on the qualitative results, theories might be developed from which hypotheses could be deduced and subsequently tested by quantitative research.

C. When the subjects belong to a culture that is closed or secretive, qualitative research should usually be favored. A skilled qualitative researcher who is willing to spend considerable time breaking through the barriers that keep researchers out is more likely to be successful than a quantitative researcher who tends to spend less time interacting with subjects.

D. When potential subjects are not available for extensive interactions or observation, the quantitative approach should be considered. For example, it might be difficult to schedule extensive interviews with chief executives of major corporations.

E. When time and funds are very limited, quantitative research might be favored. This is an arguable criterion. However, it is suggested because quantitative research can often provide a quick, inexpensive snapshot of a narrow aspect of a problem. Qualitative methods do not lend themselves to the snapshot approach.

F. When the audience (such as legislators or funding agencies) require "hard numbers," quantitative research should be favored or, at least, incorporated into a qualitative research project. When someone says, "Just the numbers, please," themes and trends illustrated with quotations are unlikely to impress. For such an audience, one should, when possible, start by presenting statistics. This might open the door to consideration of more qualitative considerations. Notice that implicit in this criterion is the notion that both qualitative and quantitative approaches might be used in a given research project, with each approach contributing a different type of information.

Up to this point, we have been considering quantitative and qualitative research as though they are opposites. However, some researchers conduct research that is a blend of the two approaches. For example, a quantitative researcher who uses semistructured interviews to collect data, reduces the data to statistics, but also reports quotations from subjects to support the statistics is conducting research that has some of the characteristics of both approaches.

As you can see, our hypothetical police commission needs to make a complex decision. How would you answer the question at the top of this page? What is the basis for your answer?

For more information on the characteristics of qualitative research, consult Appendix A.

# Exercise on Topic 10

1. Which of the following lends itself more to quantitative research?
   A. How are the social relations of adolescents who use illicit drugs different from those who do not use them?
   B. How do school attendance and grades earned in school differ between adolescents who use illicit drugs and those who do not use them?

2. Which of the following lends itself more to qualitative research?
   A. What are the differences between the social interactions of college students on commuter campuses and students on campuses where most students live on campus?
   B. To what extent does family income predict whether a student will choose to attend a commuter college or a college where most students live on campus?

3. Suppose you want to do research on a terrorist group. Which type of researcher is more likely to gain access to the subjects?

4. If little is known about a new topic, which type of research is recommended for initial use?

5. For which type of research must subjects usually be available for extensive interactions with researchers?

6. Which type of research is more suitable for getting a quick snapshot of a problem?

## Questions for Discussion

7. How would you answer the two questions in the last paragraph of this topic?

8. Suppose a team of researchers wants to conduct research to identify the characteristics of professors whom students perceive as being excellent. Would you advise them to do qualitative or quantitative research? Why?

9. Name a problem in your field of study that probably would lend itself more to the quantitative than the qualitative approach.

## For Students Who Are Planning Research

10. In light of the information in this topic, have you changed your mind about your answer to question 10 in the Exercise on Topic 9? Explain.

# TOPIC 11   PROGRAM EVALUATION

Consider a school that receives a foundation grant for a new program that emphasizes parental involvement and shared decision making. In this program, decisions are made by an administrator with the advice and consent of both teachers and parents. The ultimate purpose is to help students improve in a variety of academic and social skills. Granting agencies almost always require a report on the implementation and effectiveness of such a project. To prepare the report, we conduct **program evaluation**, also called *evaluation research*.

At first glance, it might appear that we should conduct *experimental research*, which, as you may recall from earlier topics, is a study in which we give treatments (in this case, a program) in order to determine their effects. Indeed, while elements of an evaluation effort resemble experimental work, there are some major differences.

First, program evaluation is almost always *applied research*, that is, research in which we wish to apply the findings directly to such practical decisions as whether to continue funding the program and whether to modify it. Experimental research, on the other hand, is more often than not *basic research* in which we are attempting to understand underlying theories that explain behavior. Of course, those who plan programs should be thoroughly familiar with basic research and use its tenets when planning their programs.

Second, new programs are, or should be, based on a *needs assessment*. A needs assessment is nonexperimental research in which we try to determine the needs of those who will be served by the program. For a school-based program, we might ask questions such as, "What types of skills do the students need to acquire?" and "What types of program interventions to promote these skills will be most readily accepted by students, parents, and teachers?" Pure experimental research is seldom preceded by a formal needs assessment.

Third, the programs, which are analogous to treatments in an experiment, are usually subject to *change during the course of the evaluation*. For example, perhaps a program is designed to give teachers a major role in decision making — with only a minor role for parents. If, in midstream, it is found that parental involvement is not as high as desired, adjustments may be made to give parents more of a voice in decision making. Although it is almost unheard of for a researcher to make changes in the nature of a treatment during the course of an experiment, skilled program managers are open to such modifications. In fact, program evaluators collect information during the course of a program that assists in the process of modifying the program while it is being implemented. Collecting this information is called **formative evaluation**.

Formative evaluation has two prongs. First, information is collected on the *process* of implementing a program. For example, when looking at the process, we might ask, "Were the parents notified of the program in a timely manner?" and "Were the proposed meetings of parents and teachers conducted?" These questions clearly ask about the process — not the ultimate goals of student improvement. The second prong of formative evaluation involves collecting information on the *progress toward the ultimate goals*. For example, periodic tests might be administered to see if students are showing signs of improvement. If not, evaluators and program administrators might rethink the process they are implementing and make appropriate changes. By looking at *progress*, those responsible for the program often can prevent disappointment in the final results.

When evaluators collect information about students' attainment of the ultimate goals at the end of the program (such as at the end of a school year or some other period), the activity is called **summative evaluation**. A summative evaluation report contains information about the final or long-term benefits of the program for its ultimate clients — in this case, the students. Summative evaluation often involves a comparison with a control group. For example, students in a program might be compared with similar students in other schools who are not in the program.

As you can see, program evaluation is a complex, specialized form of applied research.

# EXERCISE ON TOPIC 11

1. Is program evaluation or experimental research almost always *applied research*?

2. Is a needs assessment associated with experimental research or program evaluation?

3. Is it acceptable for a researcher to modify the treatments (programs) during the course of a program evaluation?

4. Suppose, as part of a program evaluation, an evaluator asks, "How many children were reading at grade level by the end of the program?" Is this question relevant to formative or summative evaluation?

5. Suppose, as part of a program evaluation, an evaluator asks, "Are the clients in the job placement program writing better resumes?" Is this question relevant to formative or summative evaluation?

6. Suppose, as part of a program evaluation, an evaluator asks, "Were key program personnel hired on time?" Is this question relevant to formative or summative evaluation?

7. When we look at the process of implementing a program, are we conducting summative or formative evaluation?

8. Is examining program participants' progress toward attaining the ultimate goals of the program part of summative or formative evaluation?

9. Is the attainment of the final goals for participants a subject for summative or formative evaluation?

## Questions for Discussion

10. Suppose you were on a foundation board that was giving a grant for a program to a social welfare agency. Would you prefer to have the program evaluated by an employee of the program (such as the program director) or by an external, independent evaluator? Why?

11. Sometimes programs are funded again despite negative summative evaluations. Speculate on some of the reasons for this. Are any of the reasons justifiable?

## For Students Who Are Planning Research

12. Will you be evaluating a program in your research? If yes, name the program and indicate whether you will be conducting both formative and summative research.

# TOPIC 12  ETHICAL CONSIDERATIONS IN RESEARCH

When planning research, it is imperative to consider potential harm to subjects that might result from their participation. Clearly, there is potential harm from certain treatments that we might wish to administer in experimental studies. For example, a research psychologist might expose an experimental group to an anxiety-provoking stimulus in a study designed to advance a theory of the sources and effects of anxiety. Harm might result if some subjects suffer mental anguish as a result.

Subjects also might be harmed in nonexperimental studies. For example, the process of exploring sensitive traits (such as relationships with abusive parents) might cause subjects to focus on them, leading to anxiety, sleeplessness, and so on.

Because of such potential problems, the research community has developed a body of ethical values regarding the use of humans as subjects. The primary value is that subjects must be *protected from both physical and psychological harm*. Unfortunately, it is not always possible to anticipate all the potential for harm, especially when using new treatments or measuring tools. Because of this, most universities and large school districts have research committees that review research plans for potential harm to subjects.

Another important value is that subjects *have a right to privacy*. For example, many agree that it would be a violation of parents' rights to privacy for researchers to question children about discord between the parents without parental consent even if the results might be very useful to educators, sociologists, psychologists, and others.

A related value is that subjects have a right to have the data collected about them as individuals kept *confidential*. Even if subjects freely and knowingly provide information to researchers, the researchers have an obligation not to disclose the information to others—unless the identities of the subjects are disguised or made impossible to determine by using statistics such as group averages.

Also, most researchers agree that subjects have a right to *knowledge of the purpose* of the research before they participate. Having this knowledge, they are in a better position to determine whether they wish to participate.

A key to promoting these values is *informed consent*. To use informed consent, we inform the subjects of (a) the general purpose of the research, (b) what will be done to them during the research, (c) what the potential benefit to them and others might be, (d) what the potential for harm to them might be, and (e) the fact that they may withdraw at any time, even while a study is being conducted, without penalty. This information should be provided in writing and the subjects (or their guardians) should sign that they understand it.

Another key is to *debrief* subjects after their participation in a study. Debriefing consists of reviewing the purpose(s) of the study and the procedures used and offering to share the results when they become available. It should also include reassurances that the data will remain confidential. Ideally, subjects should be allowed to ask for information about any aspect of the study. During debriefing, a researcher should be on the alert for subjects who may need more help in overcoming unanticipated harm to them than a standard debriefing session provides.

The complex process of protecting subjects from harm is made more difficult when we believe that complete honesty with potential subjects may make it impossible to study an important topic. For example, suppose we want to study the influence of lobbyists on a group of state legislators. We might get some of them to allow us to "shadow" them (that is, follow them around unobtrusively) if we present the purpose as "to understand the state's political process." How many legislators (especially those who allow themselves to be unduly influenced) would agree to being shadowed if we reveal the true purpose? Is it ethical to present only a general purpose that does not reveal our specific goal when a topic is important? Do public servants have a right to privacy? These types of questions illustrate the difficulties in balancing the need to protect subjects with the need to collect information of benefit to society.[1]

---

[1]For more information on this topic, refer to *Ethical Principles in the Conduct of Research with Human Subjects* published by the American Psychological Association.

# Exercise on Topic 12

1. Should researchers take steps to prevent psychological harm as well as physical harm to subjects?

2. Should subjects be told that they are free to withdraw from a study at any time without penalty?

3. Under the principle of informed consent, is it acceptable to hide the general purpose of a study from the subjects?

4. Should informed consent be in writing?

5. Is debriefing done before or after a study is conducted?

6. What does debriefing cover?

7. Should information about subjects be kept confidential even if the subjects freely provided it to researchers?

## Questions for Discussion

8. How would you answer the last two questions posed at the end of the previous page?

9. Suppose a researcher wants to keep a class of third-grade students in from recess to administer an attitude toward school scale to them. The purpose is to help teachers understand their students' attitudes and how they might affect students' achievement. Is there potential for harm in this case? Would it be wise to seek informed consent from the parents? Why? Why not?

10. A researcher interviews adults on their sex lives with their informed consent. During the course of the interviews, some subjects name other individuals who have not provided informed consent. Does this raise ethical concerns? What, if anything, can the researcher do to protect the other individuals?

11. Suppose one of your instructors asked you to be a subject in a research project, but did not tell you the purpose of the research or what would be done to you. Would you ask for information on these points before deciding whether to participate? Would you feel pressured to participate because the researcher was your instructor?

## For Students Who Are Planning Research

12. Do you anticipate that your study has the potential to harm the participants? If yes, what measures will you take to mitigate the potential for harm?

13. Will you be obtaining informed consent? Will you have your consent form reviewed by your professor? By a university committee? By others? Explain.

# TOPIC 13 THE ROLE OF THEORY IN RESEARCH

A **theory** is a unified explanation for discrete observations that might otherwise be viewed as unrelated or contradictory. One of the most widely studied theories in learning is reinforcement theory. It defines positive reinforcement as something that increases the frequency of the response that occurred before reinforcement was administered. Most of us have given praise as a reward to a dog for sitting. To the extent that the praise increases the sitting behavior, it constitutes positive reinforcement.

At first, reinforcement theory sounds obvious and, in a way, is self-defining. So why has it been so carefully studied? Because it explains many apparently contradictory observations. For example, suppose, at first, we praise a dog regularly for sitting and, after a while, become lax and offer praise intermittently. Common sense might tell us to expect the sitting behavior to decrease with the decrease in praise. Yet, we might actually observe an increase in sitting because reinforcement theory indicates that intermittent reinforcement[1] is, in many circumstances, more effective than consistent reinforcement. Thus, reinforcement theory is a unified set of principles that help explain why certain behaviors increase in their frequency. Without it, we would observe behaviors that do not seem to be consistent or related to each other.

One of the major functions of research is to test hypotheses derived from theory. To do this, we *deduce* hypotheses that are consistent with the theory. For example, an axiom of self-regulated learning theory states that the goals students adopt determine their level of cognitive engagement. From this, we might deduce that when students know that they will be tested again on the same material, those who have lower goals (for example, a goal of getting 70% right) should ask for less feedback about wrongly answered test items than those who have higher goals.[2] A study that confirms this hypothesis lends support to the theory. Assuming the study is methodologically strong and replicated, failure to confirm a hypothesis calls the theory (or parts of it) into question, leading theorists to consider reformulating it to account for the discrepancy.

Another major function of research is to provide the observations and conclusions on which we can *induce* theory. That is, we try to develop a theory that explains events we have observed. Anthropologists and others who practice qualitative research often refer to this as *grounded theory*— theory that is grounded on observations.[3] Grounded theory is often thought of as evolutionary. That is, it usually is developed during the process of making observations, and it is regularly revised as new observations warrant.

The desire by scientists to develop theories on all aspects of human experience should not be surprising. Unified explanations of phenomena are clearly more useful than a collection of unrelated facts collected via research methods.

If you are looking for a research topic for a thesis or term project, you would be well advised to consider a theory of interest to you. Testing some aspect of it makes a potential contribution to our understanding of all aspects of behavior related to the theory. In addition, you will find it easier to defend your selection of a research topic and to write the introduction to your research report if you can show that your study has implications for an important theory.

When thinking about theory as a basis for research, keep in mind that no theory of human behavior is universal — that is, there almost always are exceptions to the rule. This is why we usually examine *trends across groups* in order to test or develop theories. However, do not overlook the possibility of designing a study specifically to examine those individuals who do not perform as predicted by a theory. Understanding how the dynamics of their behavior differ from those who act

---

[1]For the sake of this discussion, the technical terms for various schedules of reinforcement are not discussed here.
[2]For detailed information on this topic, see Butler, D. L. & Winne, P. H. (1995). Feedback and self-regulated learning: A theoretical synthesis. *Review of Educational Research, 65,* 245–280.
[3]See Glaser, B. & Strauss, A. (1967). *The Discovery of Grounded Theory.* Chicago: Aldine.

in the way predicted by theory may help in refining a theory to take account of exceptions.

# Exercise on Topic 13

1. How is a *theory* defined in this topic?

2. Do we use induction or deduction to derive a hypothesis from a theory?

3. What are the two major functions of research mentioned in this topic?

4. If a hypothesis derived from a theory is not confirmed, what implications does this have for the theory?

5. Is grounded theory based on induction or deduction?

6. Is grounded theory a tradition in qualitative or quantitative research?

## Question for Discussion

7. Examine the discussion of a theory in a textbook in your field. Does the author of the textbook cite research that supports it? Does he or she suggest unresolved issues relating to the theory that might be explored in future research? Explain.

## For Students Who Are Planning Research

8. Is the purpose of your research to test a hypothesis deduced from a theory? Explain.

9. Is the purpose of your research to induce theory (i.e., make observations on which a theory may be built)?

10. Will you be conducting research without reference to theory? (Note that it is possible to plan and conduct research on practical matters without explicit reference to theory. For example, suppose your local schools went on double shifts because of overcrowding, and you want to investigate the effects of the double shifts on students' attitudes and achievement. While there may be several theories that relate to this situation, you might conduct your reseach *as a practical, nontheoretical matter* in order to better inform decision makers and taxpayers on this matter.) If you will not be referencing theory, will the results of your research still have important implications? Explain.

# PART B

## REVIEWING LITERATURE

Reviewing the research conducted by others is the first step in planning a new research project. In this part, we will first explore the reasons for reviewing literature—how it will help you identify a suitable idea for research and help you select research tools and methods. Second, we will examine how to locate literature electronically via computer. Since it is assumed that you already know how to locate books and articles in mass circulation periodicals and newspapers, the emphasis here is on how computerized databases can make your search of academic journals more efficient and precise. Finally, we will consider some basic principles for writing literature reviews.

# NOTES

# TOPIC 14  REASONS FOR REVIEWING LITERATURE

If you are planning your first research project for a class assignment or a thesis, start by identifying a broad problem area. This could be a practical problem such as "the education of bilingual children" or "dependence on welfare," or it could be a more theoretical one such as "how valid is attribution theory in informal learning situations?" The second step is to review literature on the topic. Examining both the theoretical and research literature on a topic usually will help you identify a testable hypothesis of limited scope—limited so that it can be tested within a reasonable amount of time and with the resources you have available.[1]

If you are having difficulty in identifying a research hypothesis, you might consider *replicating* a study that has already been published.[2] In a *strict replication*, we try to mimic the original study in all important respects; the purpose is to see if the same types of results will emerge. Of course, a strict replication should be undertaken only on studies with potentially important implications.

Another possibility is to locate an important study and conduct a *modified replication*, that is, a replication with some major modification(s) such as examining a new population or using an improved measurement technique. Notice, though, that if the study fails to replicate, you won't know whether it is because the original study was in error or because your modifications changed the nature of the study.

Because there are many topics on which the results of published research are conflicting, a third possibility is to plan a study designed to resolve a conflict. Published reviews of research often point out such conflicts and offer possible explanations of them; this is illustrated in the excerpts from reviews of research that are reproduced in Appendix B.

After reviewing research, you may arrive at a creative idea that is *not* a direct extension of existing research. While there are important cases of this in the history of science, they are rare. It is extremely unlikely that a novice researcher will have such an insight at the beginning of his or her career.

In addition to helping you identify testable hypotheses, reviewing published research provides other benefits. First, you may identify measuring tools (called *instruments*) that were used successfully by other researchers and, also, avoid those found to be seriously flawed. Second, you may be able to avoid dead ends; one of your ideas for research may have already been thoroughly investigated and shown to be not useful. Third, you can learn how to write research reports by paying careful attention to the style and organization used by authors of published research. To do this, do not read just for content—also notice how research reports are written.

When you write a research report, you will be expected to cite relevant research. When writing for journals, integrate the literature into your introduction. In theses and dissertations, you probably will be required to present your literature review in a separate chapter immediately following the introduction. A well-crafted review of research shows your readers the context within which you were working. It also can help to justify your study if you use it to establish the importance of your topic and to show how your research flows from that of others.

Finally, your review of research allows you to demonstrate to your instructors, thesis committee members, and others that you were able to locate research relevant to your hypothesis, to use it in planning your research, and to cite it appropriately in your review of literature.

In the next section, we'll explore how to search for literature electronically and, in the following one, we'll consider how to organize it.

---

[1]See Topic 7 to review hypotheses as well as purposes and questions, which are alternatives to hypotheses as the heart of research. A testable hypothesis is one that can be tested through direct observation.
[2]Check with your professor to see if this is acceptable in light of the objectives for the course.

# Exercise on Topic 14

1. When planning research, should you first identify a broad problem area or develop a testable hypothesis?

2. Suppose you conducted a replication of a study but used a sample from a population different from the one that was used in the first study. What type of replication did you conduct?

3. In light of this topic, should you be surprised if you find conflicting results in the research literature?

4. "According to this topic, students would be wise to try to find a creative, new research idea to explore in their first research project." Is this statement true or false?

5. In journal articles, the literature review is usually integrated into which part of the article?

6. How can you use a review of literature to help justify a study you have undertaken?

7. According to the topic, in how many ways can a review of literature help you in addition to helping you identify testable hypotheses?

## Questions for Discussion

8. The three possibilities for identifying a research project described in the topic are to conduct a strict replication, a modified replication, and a study designed to resolve a conflict in the results of published research. Are any likely to be of greater benefit to science than any of the others? Explain.

9. This topic refers you to Appendix B. Comment on each one. Are they well written? Explain

## For Students Who Are Planning Research

10. Have you begun reading the literature on your problem area? If yes, are you planning a strict replication of a previous study? A modified replication? A study that might resolve a conflict in the literature? Explain.

11. Was your research purpose or hypothesis explicitly suggested in the literature you have read?

Increasingly, students are being given direct access to electronic databases in academic libraries. In this topic, we will consider how to use them to locate articles in academic journals.

We'll explore some of the important principles for locating literature electronically (via computer) from three major sources: (1) *Sociofile*, which contains the print versions of *Sociological Abstracts* and *Social Planning/Policy & Development Abstracts*, covering journal articles published in over 1,600 journals; (2) *PsycLIT*, which contains the print version of *Psychological Abstracts*, with abstracts to journal articles worldwide since 1974[1]; and (3) *ERIC*, which contains abstracts to articles in education found in more than 600 journals from 1966 to date.[2] The following characteristics are true of all three databases.

First, for each journal article, there is a single *record*; a record contains all the information about a given article. Within each record, there are separate *fields* such as the title field, the author field, the abstract (that is, summary of the article) field, and the descriptor field.

A descriptor is a key subject-matter term; for example *learning environments*, *learning disabilities*, and *learning theories* are descriptors in *ERIC*. One of the important ways to access the databases is to search for articles using appropriate descriptors. To determine which descriptors are available, each database has a *Thesaurus*. It is important to refer to it to identify the terms you wish to use in your search. For example, if your topic is *group therapy* for *child molesters*, the appropriate descriptors in *PsycLIT* are *group-psychotherapy* and *pedophilia*.

The following are some principles for conducting a search. First, we can search a particular field or search entire records. If you have identified appropriate descriptors in the *Thesaurus*, it is usually sufficient to search the descriptors fields using the descriptors.[3]

We can conduct a search for all articles containing either (or both) of two descriptors by using *OR*. For example, the instruction to find "dyslexia" *OR* "learning disabilities" will locate all articles with either one of these descriptors. Thus, using *OR* broadens our search.

We can also broaden our search by using a root word such as *alcohol* followed by an asterisk (*); the asterisk instructs the program to search for the plural form as well as derivatives such as *alcoholism* and *alcoholics*.

Frequently, we wish to narrow our search in order to make it more precise. An important instruction for doing this is *AND*. For instance, if we use the instruction to locate articles with "*learning environments AND dyslexia*," the program will only identify articles with *both* these descriptors and exclude articles that have only one of them.

We can also make our search more precise by using *NOT*. The instruction "*advertising NOT television*" will identify all articles relating to advertising but exclude any that relate to advertising on television.

If you are working in a field with thousands of references, you can be more precise by adding another search concept such as age group (child, adolescent, adult, or elderly) and population (human or animal).

If you are required to use only recent references, you can also limit the search to recent years.

Other important indices for locating journal articles are described in Appendix C.

---

[1]Use the print version for journal articles published before 1974.

[2]The emphasis in this topic is on journal articles. Note that *PsycLIT* also abstracts books, *Sociofile* also abstracts dissertations, and *ERIC* also abstracts unpublished documents such as convention papers, which are available on microfiche.

[3] If you are not able to find appropriate descriptors, conduct a "free text" search, using your own terms (such as *child molester*, which is not a *Thesaurus* term) and searching entire records. If this term appears in any field in any of the records, the record(s) will be selected. If any are selected, examine the descriptors field to see what descriptors have been assigned to it — noticing *pedophilia*, you could now search again looking only in the descriptors field for the *Thesaurus* descriptor, *pedophilia*.

# EXERCISE ON TOPIC 15

1. What is the name of the database used primarily by psychologists?

2. What is the name of the database used primarily by educators?

3. Does a *record* or a *field* contain all the information about a given article?

4. What feature of the databases discussed in the topic helps you determine what descriptors are used in the database?

5. When should you use *OR*?

6. Does using *AND* narrow or broaden a search?

7. Does using *NOT* narrow or broaden a search?

8. What does an asterisk after a root word do to the search?

9. If we search for *discipline AND rewards*, will we retrieve more references than if we searched using each term separately?

## Question for Discussion

10. If you have searched for journal articles electronically in the past, briefly describe your experience(s). Was it easy to do? What suggestions do you have for others who will be doing it for the first time?

## For Students Who Are Planning Research

11. Name some *descriptors* that you might use in an electronic search of the literature. Have you checked in a thesaurus to see if they are valid for use in the database you plan to access? Explain.

# TOPIC 16  WRITING LITERATURE REVIEWS

Usually, the first thing you should do in a literature review is to name and describe your broad problem area and provide conceptual definitions of major terms if you believe your audience may not know their meanings.[1]

The second step usually is to establish the importance of your topic. One way to do this is to show that your topic was deemed important enough to be investigated by others as illustrated in Example 1, which is the first two paragraphs in the introduction to an article by Nail, MacDonald, and Levy (2000).

EXAMPLE 1

Social influence is central to the field of psychology. In fact, social psychology can almost be defined as the study of social influence (Jones, 1985; for reviews, see Allen, 1965; Cialdini & Trost, 1998; Levine & Russo, 1987; Maass & Clark, 1984; Wood, Lundgren, Ouellette, Busceme, & Blackstone, 1994). Social influence refers to any situation in which a person's thoughts, feelings, or behaviors are affected by the real or imagined presence of one or more others (Allport, 1985).

Numerous research paradigms have been employed in the study of social influence. Some of the major paradigms include. . . . (p. 454)[2]

Note that you may also establish the importance of a topic by citing statistics that indicate how many people are affected by a particular problem (e.g., how many cases of rape were reported last year) or how many people are in the population of interest (e.g., how many children enrolled in special classes for the gifted). Some of the major sources for statistics are described in Appendix D.

The next step is to write a *topic-by-topic* description of relevant research, and provide major and minor subheadings to guide readers through a long literature review. For example, some of the **major** and *minor* subheadings used by Reis, Collins, & Berscheid (2000) in their review of research on the influence of social relationships on human development are: **Conceptualization of Relationships** (*The Concept of Relationship, Types of Relationships, Cultural Variations in Relationships*), **The Role of Relationships in Human Survival and Well Being** (*Innate Social Response Systems, Face Perception, Attachment*).[3]

When citing literature on each topic, group references together when they have something in common. Also, when there are varying viewpoints on an issue, point them out. These principles are followed by Orlando, Ellickson, & Jinnett (2001) in Example 2.

EXAMPLE 2

Researchers studying tobacco use and emotional distress in adolescents have proposed that psychological risk factors such as difficult family situations or a tendency toward risk taking underlie both phenomena (Covey & Tam, 1990; Escobedo et al., 1998; Kaplan, Landa, Weinhold, & Shenker, 1984). A longitudinal study of adult twins points to the existence of a genetic predisposition to both depressive symptomatology and a propensity to use tobacco (Kendler et al., 1993). In addition, Breslau et al. (1998) suggested that a personality disorder such as neuroticism may be driving both tobacco use and emotional distress. (p. 959)[4]

Also note that you should indicate the *results* of the research you are citing, as was done in Example 2; do not just describe the research methodology. In fact, it is often not necessary to discuss methodology; should you elect not to do so, your readers are likely to assume that you believe it

---

[1]See Topic 8 for a discussion of the differences between conceptual and operational definitions. Conceptual definitions may also be integrated throughout a literature review as new terms are introduced.

[2]Source: Nail, P. R., MacDonald, G., & Levy, D. A. (2000). Proposal of a four-dimensional model of social response. *Psychological Bulletin, 126,* 454–470.

[3]Source: Reis, H. T., Collins, W. A., & Berscheid, E. (2000). The relationship context of human behavior and development. *Psychological Bulletin, 126,* 844–872.

[4]Source: Orlando, M., Ellickson, P. L., & Jinnett, K. (2001). *Journal of Consulting and Clinical Psychology, 69,* 959–970.

was reasonably strong. Thus, if you hold the opposite belief, you might want to point out specific weaknesses with statements such as: "In a preliminary pilot study with 14 registered nurses as subjects, Doe and Smith (1996) found . . . ."

Sometimes it is appropriate to trace the history of a topic by describing the first important article on it and tracing how theories on it evolved as more evidence became available. A search of the *Social Sciences Citation Index* (see Appendix C) will help greatly if you want to do this.

At the end of a long review of literature, it is appropriate to summarize the review, with attention to how the review relates to your study. For example, you might point out that there are contradictions in the research, which your research might help resolve. You might also point out gaps in the literature that your study might help fill.

# EXERCISE ON TOPIC 16

1. According to the topic, what is the first thing one should usually do in a literature review?

2. Should you organize a literature review around topics or around important authors on the area of investigation?

3. What two ways are suggested for showing the importance of your topic?

4. Should references that have something in common be grouped together or discussed separately in a literature review?

5. Is it appropriate to indicate the results of the research being cited?

6. If you do not discuss the research methodology used in references you are citing in a literature review, what are your readers likely to assume?

7. According to the topic, is it ever appropriate to cite older references in a literature review? Why?

## Questions for Discussion

8. Novice researchers sometimes write a summary of each publication they wish to cite and then string the summaries together, one after the other. They then consider their string of summaries as an effective literature review. What are the weaknesses of this approach?

9. Students usually are expected to cite more references in masters theses than they would be expected to cite when writing a journal article, even if it is an article for a major, prestigious journal. Speculate on the reason(s) for this.

## For Students Who Are Planning Research

10. Name some of the major and minor subheadings that you anticipate you might use to organize your literature review. (Note that these might change after you have read the literature on your topic.)

# Part C

## Sampling

When it is impractical to study an entire population, we draw a sample, study it, and infer that what is true of the sample is probably true of the population. Since inferences to a population are only as good as the method used to draw the sample, we will explore the advantages and disadvantages of various methods of sampling in detail. The issue of sample size is also discussed in detail in this part.

# NOTES

# TOPIC 17  BIASED AND UNBIASED SAMPLING

We frequently draw a **sample** from a **population**, which is the group in which we are ultimately interested. A population may be large, such as all social workers in the United States, or small, such as all social workers employed by a specific hospital. If we study every member of a population, we are conducting a **census**. For large populations, however, it is more efficient to study a sample instead of conducting a census. After drawing a sample, we study it, and then make an inference to the population—that is, we infer that the characteristics of the sample probably are the characteristics of the population.[1]

Obviously, the quality of our samples affects the quality of our inferences; a poor sample is likely to lead to incorrect inferences. The two questions we ask when evaluating a sample are: "Is the size adequate?," a question that is discussed in Topics 21 and 22, and "Is the sample biased?"

We obtain an **unbiased sample** by giving every member of a population an equal chance of being included in the sample. One way to do this is to put the names of those in the population on slips of paper and draw as many as we need for the sample. The result is a **simple random sample**.[2]

Note that we cannot give every member of a population an equal chance of being included unless we can identify all members of the population. Failure to identify all members of a population is a major source of bias in sampling. For example, if our population is all homeless people in a city, but we can identify only those who seek public assistance and those who seek food and clothing at charitable institutions, we can sample only from these select members of the population. But what about the less visible homeless? They may be less resourceful, more destitute (or less destitute), more recently made homeless, and so on. Our sample is biased against them, and our inferences about all homeless people will be incorrect to the extent that they are numerous in the population and are different from those who are accessible.

We also obtain biased samples when we use **samples of convenience** (also known as *accidental samples*). For example, if a psychology professor wants to study a principle of learning theory as it applies to all college sophomores, but only uses those students who happen to be enrolled in her introductory psychology class, the sample is biased against all other college sophomores. This introduces many possibilities for error. For example, the professor may have a reputation for being easy and, thus, attracts to her classes students with learning styles that are different from those of the general population of college sophomores.

A third major source of bias is **volunteerism**. Volunteerism takes two forms. First, sometimes we simply issue a call for volunteers. This is often done in medical research in which researchers advertise for potential subjects, such as those with chronic heart conditions, in order to test new methods of treatment. What's wrong with this? The possibilities are endless. For example, some people may volunteer because they are becoming desperate as their condition worsens, whereas those who are doing better may be less inclined to expose themselves to experimental treatment, *or* those who volunteer may be more persistent and resourceful (and, thus in better health) than the general population of those with heart conditions. These two opposing possibilities illustrate why we are eager to eliminate bias—because we usually don't know the direction in which it affects our results.

Second, volunteerism also may bias a sample even if we begin by identifying a random sample. For example, we might draw a random sample of all freshmen at a college and contact them to take part in a study of attitudes toward technology in higher education. For a variety of reasons, many of those in the random sample we have selected may refuse to participate. Those who participate, in effect, are volunteers and may be fundamentally different from nonvolunteers—such as being more interested in technology and more concerned about their education.

---

[1]The process of *inferring* from a sample to a population is also called *generalizing*.
[2]Another method for drawing a simple random sample is described in the next topic.

# Exercise on Topic 17

1. In the topic, how is *population* defined?

2. If we study every member of a population, what type of study are we conducting?

3. How can we draw an unbiased sample?

4. Suppose we draw a random sample from a population of college students, but some of those selected refuse to take part in our study. Are those who participated in our study a biased or unbiased sample of the population?

5. If you mail questionnaires to all clients of a social worker, and 50% of them are completed and returned, is your sample biased or unbiased?

6. Suppose a psychologist has her clients participate in an experiment she is conducting because they are accessible to her. What type of sample is she using?

7. Briefly describe one way we can draw a simple random sample.

## Questions for Discussion

8. People who receive questionnaires in the mail often fail to return them, creating a bias because those who do return them are volunteers. Speculate on some things a researcher can do to get more people to respond by thinking about questionnaires you have received in the past.

9. Are you convinced by the text that researchers should go to great lengths to avoid bias in their samples? Why? Why not?

10. Suppose you drew a random sample of all licensed clinical psychologists in your community and wished to survey them by phone. On the days that you made the phone calls, some of them were not available to be interviewed, so you drew replacements for them at random from the population of licensed clinical psychologists. Speculate on whether the sample is biased or unbiased in light of the fact that replacements were drawn at random.

## For Students Who Are Planning Research

11. Do you anticipate you will be drawing a sample for your study or will you be conducting a census?

12. If you will be sampling, do you anticipate that you will be using a biased sample? If yes, what do you anticipate will be the source of the bias? Is there anything you can do to reduce the bias? Explain.

# TOPIC 18  SIMPLE RANDOM AND SYSTEMATIC SAMPLING

As you know from the previous section, a **simple random sample** is one in which we give every member of a population an equal chance of being included in a sample. Putting names on slips of paper and drawing them from a hat is one way to obtain such a sample. A preferable method is to use a table of random numbers, a portion of which is reproduced in Table 1 on page 131 of this book. It consists of numbers that are unrelated to each other or to anything else. To use such a table, you must give each member of a population a *number name*, and each name must contain the same number of digits. For example, if there are 70 members of a population, name the first person 00 (it doesn't matter who the first person is since we're just renaming, not selecting, at this point). Name the second person 01, the third person 02, etc.[1] After doing this, flip to any page in your book of random numbers (we have only one in the appendix) and, without looking, point to a number —this is the number of the first person selected. Let's assume that the first number you pointed to was the first digit in the first row in Table 1, which is 2. The digit to the right of it is 1; together, they are the number 21. Thus, person number 21 has been selected. Now move two digits to the right; the next two digits (ignoring the space between them, which is there only to help guide your eye) are 0 and 4. Thus, person number 04 has been selected. The next two digits are 9 and 8. Since there are only 70 people in the population, no one is named 98. This selection does not help us, so we move on to the right. The next two digits are 0 and 8, which selects person number 08. We continue in this manner until we have the number of participants we need for the sample.[2]

It is important to note that random samples are subject to error. For example, quite by chance a random sample might contain a disproportionately large number of males, or Republicans, or high achievers, and so on. Error created by random sampling is simply called **sampling error** by statisticians. Fortunately, if we use a sample of adequate size (a topic treated later), sampling error is minimized. Also, inferential statistics help us evaluate the effects of sampling errors on our results.

Notice that bias also creates errors when sampling (see Topic 17). However, these are nonchance errors, which are not reduced by increasing sample size. For example, if you sample for a political survey and your method is biased against Republicans, increasing the sample size while using the same sampling method only gives you a larger sample of voters who tend not to be Republicans. The larger sample is no more accurate than the smaller one.

Another method of sampling that some researchers regard as being essentially equivalent to simple random sampling is **systematic sampling**. In this type of sampling, every *n*th person is selected. This can be any number such as two, in which case we select every second person.[3] This sounds easy, but there is a potential catch. Suppose someone has arranged the population in such a way that every second person is somehow different from the others. Perhaps the population has been arranged in this order: man next to woman, next to man, next to woman, and so on. If we draw every other person, we will obtain a sample of all males or all females. Because we cannot be sure that no one has ordered a list of the population in a way that might affect our sample, we usually use an alphabetical list to draw from with systematic sampling. In addition, we use a random starting point; for example, if we are going to draw every third person, we select from the first three people on the list using simple random sampling. Finally, we need to go completely through the alphabetical list—through the letter *z*—since different national origin groups tend to concentrate at different points in the alphabet. Following this procedure yields a good sample, but note that it is a systematic sample; it should *not* be referred to as a random sample because the two procedures are different.

---

[1]Notice that because the population size, 70, contains two digits, every member of the population is given a two-digit number name.

[2]Some computer programs may also be used to select random samples.

[3]Divide the population size by the desired sample size to determine the value of *n*.

# EXERCISE ON TOPIC 18

1. Is there a sequence or pattern to the numbers in a table of random numbers?

2. In the topic, you learned how to use a table of random numbers to draw what type of sample?

3. What is the name for errors created by random sampling?

4. How can we minimize sampling errors?

5. Can we minimize the effects of a bias in sampling by increasing the sample size?

6. Suppose you want to sample from a population of 99 clients and your random starting point in Table 1 is the first digit in the second row. What are the numbers of the first two clients selected?

7. Suppose you want to sample from a population of 500 clients and your random starting point in Table 1 is the first digit in the fifth row. What are the numbers of the first two clients selected?

8. If you draw every other person from a list of the population, you are using what type of sampling?

9. What is the potential problem with systematic sampling?

10. How can we get around the problem you named in answer to question 9?

## Questions for Discussion

11. Suppose a friend was planning to use simple random sampling in a research project from which she wants to generalize to all students on a campus. Would you recommend drawing names from a hat or using a table of random numbers? Why?

12. Suppose a friend predicts that candidate Smith will win a local election, and the prediction is based on the opinions expressed by his friends and neighbors. What would you say to help him understand that this method of sampling is unsound?

## For Students Who Are Planning Research

13. Do you plan to use random sampling? Systematic sampling?

14. If you answered no to both parts of question 13, explain why you will not be using one of these methods.

# TOPIC 19  STRATIFIED RANDOM SAMPLING

As you know from the previous two topics, simple random sampling gives each member of a population an equal chance of being included in a sample. The resulting sample is, by definition, *unbiased*, yet may contain *sampling errors*, which are errors created by chance (that is, at random). The technical term we use when discussing sampling error is *precision*. Our results are more precise when we reduce sampling errors.

One way we can attempt to reduce sampling errors is to draw a **stratified random sample**. To do this, we divide a population into strata. For example, we usually can easily divide a population into men and women. If we draw separately at random from each stratum, we will obtain a stratified random sample.

Before considering how stratification helps reduce sampling error, let's look at it in more detail. First, we usually draw the same percentage of participants *not* the same number of participants from each stratum.[1] Thus, if there are 600 women and 400 men in a population and if we want a sample size of 100, we would draw 10% of the women (that is, 600 x .10 = 60) and 10% of the men (that is, 400 x .10 = 40). Thus, our sample consisting of 60 women and 40 men is representative in terms of gender—that is, it accurately represents the gender composition of the population. At first, some students think that men and women should have equal representation in the sample. To illustrate why this is wrong, suppose you were trying to predict the outcome of a local election on a proposition requiring equal pricing of services such as dry cleaning for men and women. Since women are traditionally charged more, they might be more likely to vote in favor of it than men. Thus, because there are more women voters in the population, there should be more women voters in our sample. Notice, however, that if men and women do not differ in their opinions on this particular issue, stratification will not increase the precision of our result. Think about it — if men and women are the same in their opinions (perhaps 80% approve and 20% disapprove), it

does not matter if we have a sample consisting of all men, all women, or something in between since in any of these combinations we would expect 80% to approve and 20% to disapprove. In other words, the stratification variable of gender is irrelevant if those in the two strata are the same in terms of what we are studying. Thus, stratification will help us only if we stratify on a variable that is relevant.

We can further increase our precision (remember, this means reducing sampling errors) by using multiple strata in selecting a given sample. We might, for example, stratify on the basis of gender and age by drawing separate random samples from each of the four subgroups shown here:

| Women<br>Ages 18–39 | Men<br>Ages 18–39 |
|---------------------|-------------------|
| Women<br>Ages 40+   | Men<br>Ages 40+   |

To the extent that the two stratification variables are relevant to a study, they will increase precision.

Of course, we are not confined to using just two variables for stratification — more are better as long as they are relevant and *independent* of each other. To see what is meant by independence, let's suppose that we stratified on both age and number of years employed. Since older people have had more years in which to be employed, the two are probably highly correlated. Thus, stratifying on age has probably accounted to a great extent for years of employment.

Because researchers often make comparisons across age and gender subgroups, it's easy to lose sight of the primary purpose of stratification, which is to ensure that different subgroups are represented in the correct proportions. Our goal in stratification is *not* to make comparisons across subgroups. To make such comparisons, we do *not* need equal proportions since statistics such as

---

[1] If equal numbers are drawn, the responses from each stratum can be statistically weighted to make the statistical result reflect the population proportions.

group averages take care of unequal sample sizes
of the groups to be compared.

# Exercise on Topic 19

1. Our results are more *precise* when we reduce what?

2. Is it possible for a random sample to contain sampling errors?

3. What is the first step in stratified random sampling?

4. Do we usually draw the same number or the same percentage from each stratum?

5. If the population of freshmen and sophomores on your campus are the same in their opinion on an issue, will it be to your advantage to stratify by drawing samples separately from each group?

6. What does stratification do to precision?

7. Is it possible to stratify on more than one variable?

8. Is the primary purpose of stratifying to be able to compare subgroups (such as comparing freshmen and sophomores in question 5)?

## Questions for Discussion

9. Think of an issue on which you would want to conduct a survey, using the students at your college or university as the population. Name the issue and two variables you think would be relevant for stratification purposes when drawing a stratified random sample.

10. Students were given a test on which they answered questions about a research article they had read for class. One question asked, "What type of sampling was used?" Students who answered "random sampling" lost a point for the question. The instructor's comment was that the answer was ambiguous. Do you think the instructor was right in taking off the point? Why? Why not?

## For Students Who Are Planning Research

11. If you had planned to use random sampling based on Topic 18, do you now think your study would be improved if you used *stratified* random sampling instead? If yes, on what basis do you plan to stratify?

# TOPIC 20  OTHER METHODS OF SAMPLING

In the previous three topics, you learned about simple random sampling, systematic sampling, and stratified random sampling. In this topic, we'll consider several other methods.

In **cluster sampling**, we draw groups (or clusters) of participants instead of individuals. For example, suppose we want to survey a sample of members of United Methodist churches throughout the United States. If we obtain a membership list with addresses, we might draw a simple or stratified random sample of individuals and mail questionnaires to them; however, mailed questionnaires are notorious for their low response rates. We might get a better response rate if we draw a sample of clusters—in this case, congregations—and contact the ministers of them to request that they distribute the questionnaires to their members, personally collect them, and mail them back to us. If the ministers are convinced that our survey is appropriate and important, they might use their influence to help us obtain responses from the individuals in the congregations (that is, clusters) they minister to. Of course, for cluster sampling to be unbiased, we must draw the clusters *at random*.

A major drawback to cluster sampling stems from the fact that each cluster tends to be more homogeneous in a variety of ways than the population as a whole. Suppose, for example, that church members in the South tend to be more conservative than members in the North. Then, members of any one cluster in the South are unlikely to reflect accurately the attitudes of all members nationally. If we draw five clusters (that is, congregations) at random, we might obtain a large number of participants, especially if one or two have very large memberships. But by drawing only five clusters, we could easily end up with most of the churches being in the South or in the North, potentially creating much sampling error. To avoid this problem, we need to draw a large number of clusters.[1] To help with this problem, we could also stratify on geography and draw a random sample of clusters from each stratum.

Another method is **purposive** sampling. When we use this method, we purposively select those whom we believe will give us the best information as participants. For example, we might observe over a long period that several members of the academic senate at a university consistently vote on the winning side on controversial issues. We might decide that, rather than sampling at random from the whole membership, we will interview only these consistent winners to predict the outcome on a new issue. While this method is interesting and may be useful at times, it is dangerous—in this case, because professors may change their orientations or because a new issue may raise different kinds of concerns than those raised by earlier issues.

**Snowball sampling** can be useful when attempting to locate participants who are hard to find. For example, suppose you want to study heroin addicts who have never had institutional contacts—never sought treatment or had been arrested. How will you find them? With the snowball technique, you initially only need to find *one*. If you can convince this one that you have a legitimate research concern and that the data will remain confidential, he or she may put you in contact with several others. Each of these may help you contact several more. This technique is based on trust. If the initial participants trust you, they may identify and convince others to trust you also. Of course, snowball samples should be presumed to be biased, but without them, there are many special populations that we would be unable to study such as successful criminals, pedophiles, and others with something to hide.

Finally, we can use **multistage sampling**. For example, we might first draw a stratified random sample of counties in the United States (stratifying on urban, suburban, and rural status), then draw a simple random sample of households within the counties selected, and finally draw an individual from each household at random. This method is often used in large, national surveys.

---

[1]Sample size is discussed in the next topic.

45

# Exercise on Topic 20

1. To conduct a survey on a campus, a researcher drew a random sample of 25 class sections and contacted the instructors who administered the questionnaires in class. This researcher used what type of sampling?

2. Which type of sampling is based on trust between participants and a researcher?

3. If we first draw a stratified random sample of voting precincts, then draw a random sample of city blocks within the selected precincts, and then draw a random sample of households within the selected blocks, we are using what type of sampling?

4. What is a major drawback to cluster sampling?

5. Which type of sampling is useful when attempting to locate participants who are hard to find?

6. Briefly define purposive sampling.

7. What must we do in cluster sampling to obtain an unbiased sample of clusters?

8. Suppose you have identified a person who has engaged in an illegal activity to be a subject of your research, and then you identify others who have engaged in the same activity through the first person's contacts. You are using what type of sampling?

## Questions for Discussion

9. To study a sample of all nurses employed by hospitals in a state, a researcher drew two hospitals (clusters) at random, both of which happened to be large public hospitals with hundreds of nurses. Are you impressed with the sample size? Why? Why not?

10. Name a population (other than those mentioned in the topic) for which snowball sampling might be better than other types of sampling. Explain the reason for your answer.

## For Students Who Are Planning Research

11. In light of Topics 17, 18, 19, and 20, what type of sample do you plan to draw? If your sampling plan is less than entirely satisfactory to you, explain why it was necessary to draw such a sample.

# TOPIC 21  INTRODUCTION TO SAMPLE SIZE

In Topics 17 through 20, you learned about various methods of drawing samples. You should have surmised from the topics that the most important criterion when judging the adequacy of a sample is whether there is bias. Sample size is an important but secondary consideration. Let's see why with an example. Suppose you are conducting a survey on whether the main cafeteria on campus should remain open during evening hours. Being a commuter with only day classes, you go to the cafeteria at lunchtime and ask every tenth student who enters to participate in the survey.[1] Of the 100 you sample, 80% have no opinion, and 20% want evening hours. After thinking about it, you decide that maybe you should have used a larger sample, so you obtain another 100 in the same way. This time, you get 85% with no opinion, and 15% who want evening hours. Being extra cautious, you do it again and this time get a 75%–25% split. Combining results, you get the total shown here:

|           | No Opinion | Want Evening Hours |
|-----------|------------|--------------------|
| Sample 1  | 80%        | 20%                |
| Sample 2  | 85%        | 15%                |
| Sample 3  | 75%        | 25%                |
| **Total** | **80%**    | **20%**            |

Notice that for all practical purposes, the three results are the same. That is, only a small minority wants evening hours. With a total sample size of 300, you might feel rather comfortable that you have pinned down an answer close to the truth. But there's a catch, of course. Each time you sampled, you sampled only from those eating *lunch* in the cafeteria. The sample is biased against those not on campus during lunch hours — in fact, it is biased against evening students who are the members of the population most likely to want evening hours. If you continue to increase your sample size by sampling only at lunchtime, obtaining the responses of many hundreds of students, the increase in sample size will be of no benefit to you.

Clearly, you would be much better off with a smaller, unbiased sample.

As a general rule, increasing sample size increases *precision*. When we say we have precision, we are saying that the results will vary by only a small amount from sample to sample—which is what will happen if each sample is large. Notice that in our cafeteria example, the results of the three samples were reasonably close, so we might be tempted to say we have precision. But because of the bias, it would be more accurate to say that our results are *precisely wrong* to the extent that the bias has consistently thrown us off in the same direction each time we sampled.

Thus, we should strive first to obtain an unbiased sample and then seek a reasonably large number of participants.

If increasing the size of an unbiased sample increases precision, then the larger the sample the better, right? Well, yes, but there's a catch because increasing sample size produces *diminishing returns*. To understand this, consider two cases in which sample size was increased by 50 participants:

|              | Original Sample Size | Increase | New Sample Size |
|--------------|----------------------|----------|-----------------|
| Researcher A | 50                   | +50      | 100             |
| Researcher B | 3,000                | +50      | 3,050           |

If you think about it for a bit, you should realize that Researcher A will get a much bigger payoff for increasing her sample size by 50—she has doubled her sample size and gets a big boost in precision. Researcher B, on the other hand, will have little increase in precision; the addition of 50 to an original sample of 3,000 can have little influence on his results; the responses of the 50 will be overwhelmed by the first 3,000. Thus, at some point, the returns diminish to the point that it is of little use to further increase sample size. That's why even the most important and prestigious national surveys are often conducted with only about 1,500 participants.

---

[1]Selecting every *n*th person is an example of *systematic sampling* (see Topic 18).

# EXERCISE ON TOPIC 21

1. Is sample size the primary criterion when judging the adequacy of a sample?

2. Does increasing sample size reduce bias?

3. Does increasing sample size increase precision?

4. Researcher A increased his sample size from 200 to 250, and Researcher B increased her sample size from 1,000 to 1,050. Which researcher will get a bigger payoff in increased precision by adding 50 participants?

5. Does each additional subject you add to a sample make an equal contribution to increasing precision?

6. According to the topic, prestigious national surveys are often conducted with about how many participants?

## Questions for Discussion

7. A poll was conducted by a magazine editor by printing a questionnaire in an issue of the magazine for readers to mail back. Thousands of readers returned completed questionnaires. Suppose a friend reads the results and is convinced that it reflects the views of all adults. What would you say to convince him that he might be wrong?

8. Consider the statement, "The larger the sample, the better." Explain why this statement might be misleading to a novice researcher.

## For Students Who Are Planning Research

9. At this point, what is the anticipated sample size for your study? (Note that you will be learning more about sample size in the next topic.)

# TOPIC 22   A CLOSER LOOK AT SAMPLE SIZE

One of the first questions students ask when planning their theses or classroom research projects is, "How many participants do I need?" This question is often asked before a discussion of the topic and purpose of the research, but certain information is needed to determine sample size. The following are some of the major considerations.

First, researchers frequently conduct pilot studies, which are studies designed to obtain preliminary information on how new procedures and instruments work. For instance, when studying a new drug, we might conduct a pilot study to determine the route of administration and the maximum tolerable dose. We also might try out a new questionnaire to determine if there are ambiguous questions, questions that participants refuse to answer, and so on. Pilot studies are usually conducted on small samples—such as 20 to 100. Based on the results, procedures and instruments are modified for use in more definitive studies.

Second, our procedures might be expensive and time consuming—requiring us to limit our sample size. For example, when conducting qualitative research, we might plan to spend considerable time interacting with each subject, and, thus, we might have to be content with a small sample.

Third, we might wish to document the incidence of something rare such as the incidence of heart attacks among men ages 18 to 30. If we draw a small sample, such as 25 participants, and wait a year, we probably would not observe any heart attacks—but we would be wrong to conclude that there are no heart attacks in this population. For this type of work, if we cannot afford to use very large samples, we should let someone else with adequate resources do it because small samples are not useful for observing rare events.

Fourth, we need to consider the variability in our population. If there is very little variability (i.e., the population is homogeneous), we can use a small sample. For example, the population of small bags of Fritos is homogeneous with respect to their weight since the manufacturer strives to be consistent in this respect. Studying a random sample of only 50 would give us about the same information as studying a random sample of

1,000. However, if a population is very heterogeneous, we need a large sample. Suppose, for example, we want to study the rate of reading literacy among adults in a large metropolitan area. There undoubtedly is great variability—ranging from the totally illiterate to the exceptionally literate. If we draw a sample of only 50 from such a diverse group, we might not get a single illiterate in our sample.

If we are looking for small differences, we need a large sample. For example, suppose the population of female voters is just slightly more in favor of a ballot proposition than the population of male voters. In small random samples of them, the sampling errors might overwhelm the small difference—and might even produce a result in which it appears that the males are slightly more in favor. Using large samples is necessary if we wish to identify small differences.

So what is large and what is small? The answer is relative. A national public opinion poll with a few hundred respondents would be considered to have a small sample because it takes about 1,500 to get highly precise results. On the other hand, an experiment in which clients are given a new form of psychotherapy for several years might be considered to have a large sample if the sample size were a few hundred because it is traditional in this type of research to use smaller numbers of participants.

When we have a small population, Table 2 on page 132 is helpful for estimating sample size for survey work in which we want to estimate the percentage who have some trait such as holding a particular belief. Using the sample size ($n$) recommended in the table that corresponds to the population size ($N$) will usually hold our error down to about 5%—that is, the true percentage in the whole population should fall within 5% of the percentage that we obtain from the sample. For example, the table indicates that for a population of 200, we need a sample size of 132 (more than half), but for a population of 400, we need a sample size of only 196 (less than half), illustrating a practical application of the principle of diminishing returns discussed in the previous topic.

# EXERCISE ON TOPIC 22

1. What are pilot studies?

2. Do we usually use small or large samples in pilot studies?

3. If we suspect that a trait is rare in a population, should we use a small or large sample to identify the incidence of the trait?

4. In what type of study might we spend considerable amounts of time interacting with participants, and what effect might this have on sample size?

5. Suppose we suspect that there is only a very small difference in the math abilities of boys and girls at the sixth-grade level. Should we use a small or large sample to measure this difference?

6. If the members of a population are very homogeneous in their attitudes toward smoking cigarettes, would it be acceptable to use a small sample to identify the percentage who are opposed to smoking?

7. According to Table 2, if you have a population of 1,900 students in a school, what is the recommended sample size?

8. According to Table 2, if you have 130 nurses in a hospital, what is the recommended sample size?

9. What is the symbol for population size in Table 2?

## Questions for Discussion

10. Some research articles based on small samples in academic journals are characterized by their authors as being pilot studies. Do you think the publication of pilot studies is justifiable? Why? Why not?

11. Examine Table 2 carefully. Does it make sense that for small populations we need to use a larger percentage (for example, for a population of 10, we need to use 100%) than for a larger population (for example, for a population of 20,000, we need to use 1.9%)? Explain.

## For Students Who Are Planning Research

12. In light of Topics 21 and 22, what is your anticipated sample size? Explain the basis for your decision. (Note that your decision may hinge, in part, on practical matters such as the availability of participants and your financial resources.)

# PART D

# MEASUREMENT

In this section, we will examine some essentials of measurement with an emphasis on how to assess the validity of tests and measures. Reliability, which is closely linked to validity, is also explored in detail. In addition, we will consider how norm groups help us interpret scores as well as an important alternative to norm-referenced measurement—criterion-referenced measurement. Finally, the distinguishing features of measures of optimum performance and measures of typical performance will be explored.

# NOTES

# TOPIC 23  INTRODUCTION TO VALIDITY

We say that an *instrument* (that is, measuring tool) is **valid** when it measures what it is supposed to measure and performs the functions that it purports to perform. For example, consider an achievement test on the westward movement in the United States that emphasizes knowledge of facts. It is probably only modestly valid when administered to students whose instruction emphasized critical appraisal of historical evidence on that period in history. Likewise, a typing test used by an employer probably is likely to be only *partially valid* if the applicants are applying for a job that includes filing and receptionist's duties in addition to typing.

You may have already inferred that validity is *relative* to the purpose of testing. If the purpose is to measure achievement of students exposed to instruction on critical thinking, a test that measures only factual knowledge will be lacking in validity. For the purpose of measuring achievement of students exposed to instruction in which the acquisition of factual knowledge was emphasized, the same test is likely to be more valid. Thus, before we can have an intelligent discussion of the validity of a particular test, we must clearly state our purpose for testing.

You also may have inferred from the examples above that validity is a *matter of degree*. We should talk about *how valid* a test is—not *whether* it is valid. Given the imperfect state of measurement practice, it is safe to say that no test is perfectly valid.

Let's briefly explore some reasons perfect validity eludes us. First, almost all tests tap only a *sample* of the behavior underlying the constructs we are trying to measure. Consider the construct of aptitude for college (that is, having the abilities to succeed in college). College aptitude tests emphasize verbal and mathematical skills and leave untapped other skills that may be related to success such as ability to use a computer, knowledge of how to use a library, command of effective study skills, and having the maturity to persist in the face of difficulty. Even within the domains that are tapped, only a small sample of problems can be presented within a test of reasonable length; we cannot, for example, test using all possible mathematical problems. Just as when we sample subjects from a population (see Part C of this book), some samples are better than others, and all samples are subject to error.

Another reason perfect validity eludes us is that some traits that we wish to measure are inherently elusive. Consider cheerfulness. We've all known people whose cheerfulness is contagious. But how can we measure this trait in order to study it? We could ask a series of questions on how subjects interact with others in various types of contexts, how they view adversity, etc. Or we might observe subjects and rate them for cheerfulness in their interactions with others (Do they smile? Is the tone of their voice upbeat?, etc.) While these procedures might tap aspects of cheerfulness, it should be clear that they will fail to capture the *full essence* of the trait. It illustrates the old principle that often the whole is greater than the sum of its parts — but, in this case, the situation is even worse because we usually can sample only some of the parts.

The problem of elusiveness, at first glance, seems to plague those with a quantitative orientation more than those with a qualitative orientation since quantitative researchers seek to reduce elusive constructs such as cheerfulness to numerical scores. Qualitative researchers tend to measure in ways (such as unstructured interviews) that yield words to describe the extent to which traits are present. Yet, unless qualitative researchers refer to specific behaviors and events in their reports, they will fail to describe results in enough detail so that readers can picture the meanings that have been attached to the constructs. Thus, listing events, quoting subjects, and describing specific interactions, while less artificial than numerical scores, can also miss the essence of a trait — such as the feeling you get when you are with a genuinely cheerful person.

# Exercise on Topic 23

1. How is the term *instrument* defined in the topic?

2. An instrument is said to be valid when it does what?

3. Suppose we purchase a commercial reading test that is highly valid for students who receive instruction in phonics. Is it possible that it is of limited validity for students who are taught with some other method?

4. According to the topic, is it safe to say that no test is perfectly valid?

5. Tapping only a sample of the behaviors underlying the constructs we wish to measure has what effect on validity?

6. If a trait is elusive, is it *easy* or *difficult* to measure it with a high degree of validity?

## Questions for Discussion

7. Have you ever taken an achievement test in school that you thought was seriously flawed in its validity? If so, describe the test and why you believe it was lacking in validity. In your discussion, refer to the purpose of testing.

8. Name a trait that you think is *elusive* and, thus, may be difficult to measure with great validity. Be prepared to defend your answer.

9. Name a trait of interest to you. If you were to study it, would you take a qualitative or quantitative approach to measuring it? Explain why.

## For Students Who Are Planning Research

10. What types of instruments (e.g., achievement tests, personality scales, interview schedules) do you plan to use in your research?

11. Will the instruments and measurement procedures that you named in response to question 10 measure a *sample* of the behvaior underlying the construct? Have you considered how to draw the sample? Explain.

12. Measuring the ability to add one-digit numbers is *not* very elusive. Are the traits you plan to measure inherently more *elusive* than measuring this mathematics skill? Explain.

# TOPIC 24  JUDGMENTAL VALIDITY

To determine the **content validity** of an instrument, we make judgments on the appropriateness of its contents. For achievement tests, this type of validity is essential.

Suppose for a moment that you are the instructor of your research methods class and wish to build an achievement test on the material in this book through Topic 22. What steps could you take to maximize the content validity of the test? First, you need to consider the amount of testing time and the types of items. For example, you can ask many more multiple-choice items than essay items in a given amount of testing time. Let's assume you decided to write 35 multiple-choice items to be administered in a 50 minute period. You could write one item on each of the 22 topics, assuring that a broad sample of the material is covered. Then you could allocate the remaining 13 items to those topics deemed to be most important. (To be fair, you should have indicated during instruction which ones are more important than others.) Finally, you need to determine at which skill levels to measure. Will you test primarily for facts and definitions (for example, Which of the following is the definition of validity?) or for higher level skills (for example, Which of the following statements from a test manual tells us something about the content validity of the test?)?

Although the above example has been simplified, it illustrates three principles for writing achievement tests with high content validity. First, a broad sample of content is usually better than a narrow one. Second, important material should be emphasized. Third, questions should be written to measure the appropriate skills such as knowledge of facts and definitions, application of definitions to new situations, drawing inferences, making critical appraisals, and so on. Of course, the skills should be those covered in instruction. Keeping these principles in mind, you can make *judgments* of the content validity of achievement tests written by others.

Although content validity is most closely associated with achievement testing, elements of it may sometimes be applied to other types of measures. For example, if you wish to measure the broad construct called *self-concept* with a series of questions, you could consider sampling from each of the narrower constructs that constitute it such as physical self-concept, academic self-concept, sexual self-concept, and so on—assuring that a broad sample has been covered. If you believe one type of self-concept is more important than others for your research purpose (e.g., academic self-concept), you might emphasize one over the others by asking more questions about it. Finally, you need to write the questions in such a way that they elicit common, shared meanings from the examinees. To do this, you need to consider the examinees' educational levels and the meanings they are likely to attach to particular words in your questions. Will they find some too difficult to understand? Are some ambiguous in their meaning? Careful consideration of these points regarding the contents of instruments helps improve validity.

We also make judgments when we consider **face validity**. In this approach to validity, we judge whether an instrument appears to be valid *on the face of it*. In other words, on superficial inspection, does it appear to measure what it purports to measure? For example, one might use a spatial relations test for selecting people for pilot training. One that uses geometric shapes moving in space would have less face validity than one that uses miniature airplanes moving in space. That is, the second one has more face validity on the surface even though both might be equally valid for measuring the underlying ability to visualize objects moving in space. Thus, face validity is primarily a public relations concern; we usually prefer to use tests that *look like* they are related to their purpose because this promotes public acceptance of testing and motivates examinees to do their best. Thus, among two tests of equal validity as determined by other means, we usually should select the one with the higher face validity.

Occasionally, we deliberately use instruments with *low face validity*. For example, in a recent survey on the drug Viagra (a drug for the treatment of sexual dysfunction in males—a sensitive topic for some people), the pollsters asked about a variety of drugs even though they were concerned only with attitudes toward Viagra. The face validity of the survey questions was diluted with questions about other drugs in the hope of reducing the potential sensitivity of the questions on the drug of interest. In general, low face validity is desirable when we wish to disguise the true purpose of the research from the respondents. This can, of course, raise ethical issues. (See Topic 12 for information on these issues.)

# EXERCISE ON TOPIC 24

1. For what type of test is content validity essential?

2. Should we consider the types of skills required by achievement test items when judging content validity?

3. "To improve content validity, it is usually desirable to cover only a narrow sample of content from the broad content area to be covered by an achievement test." Is this statement true or false?

4. Is content validity relevant only to achievement tests?

5. Which type of validity is based on superficial inspection?

6. What two types of validity rely on judgments?

7. When might a researcher deliberately use an instrument with low face validity?

## Questions for Discussion

8. Suppose an instructor fails to tell students the types of items (for example, multiple-choice or essay) that will be on a midterm examination. Could this affect the validity of the results? Explain.

9. Have you ever taken an achievement test in which the content that was emphasized was different from the content you concentrated on while studying for the test? If so, describe the discrepancy and speculate on what caused it (for example, was there a miscommunication between you and the instructor?).

10. Is it logically possible for a test to have high face validity but low content validity? Explain.

## For Students Who Are Planning Research

11. Will you be considering the content validity of any instruments you will be using in your research? Explain.

12. Will your instrument(s) have face validity? Explain.

# TOPIC 25  EMPIRICAL VALIDITY

In the empirical[1] approach to validity, we make planned comparisons to see if a measure yields scores that relate to a *criterion*. To see what this means, let's consider an example:

EXAMPLE 1

A new employment test was administered to nine applicants for the position as clerk-typist; it yielded scores from 15 to 35. All nine were hired, and after six months on the job, they were rated on their job performance by their supervisors on a scale from 10 (excellent performance) to 1. Here are their scores and ratings:

| Employee | Test Score | Supervisors' Ratings | |
|----------|-----------|---------------------|---|
| Joe | 35 | 9 | |
| Jane | 32 | 10 | Top third on test. |
| Bob | 29 | 8 | |
| June | 27 | 8 | |
| Leslie | 25 | 7 | Middle third on test. |
| Homer | 22 | 8 | |
| Milly | 21 | 6 | |
| Jake | 18 | 4 | Bottom third on test. |
| John | 15 | 5 | |

In Example 1, the test scores are being validated by being compared to supervisors' ratings. The set of ratings is called the *criterion* (or standard) by which the test is being judged. Since the purpose of an employment test is to *predict* success on the job, the most appropriate test of its validity is **predictive validity**—to what extent does the test predict what it is supposed to predict?

So how valid is the employment test in Example 1? We can begin to answer the question by examining the table. First, notice that those in the bottom third on the test are also in the bottom third in terms of ratings, suggesting that the test is highly valid for identifying those who get low ratings on the job. Next, notice that the results for the top and middle thirds are more mixed. For example, Bob, who is in the top third on the test with a score of 29, has the same rating as two of the people in the middle third of the test. Thus, while the test has some validity at these levels, it is less than perfectly valid.

We can get more information on the test's predictive validity if we look at the rank order of individuals on the test in comparison to their rank order on the ratings. In Example 1, the individuals are already ordered from high to low in terms of test scores. However, the order on ratings is to some extent similar but not the same. For example, Joe has the highest test score, but only the second highest rating; Leslie is higher than Homer on the test, but Homer is higher than Leslie on the ratings. Despite exceptions such as these, the overall ordering of individuals by the test is similar to the ordering in terms of ratings.

A third way to look at a test's predictive validity is to compute its *validity coefficient*. A validity coefficient is a *correlation coefficient* used to express validity. Correlation coefficients are described in detail in Topic 47. At this point, we'll just consider some basic properties of validity coefficients. In practice, they range from 0.00 to 1.00.[2] At the upper limit, a 1.00 indicates perfect validity—you may think of this as indicating that the ranks on the test are identical to the ranks on the criterion. At the lower limit, 0.00 indicates that there is no relationship between the ranks on the test and the ranks on the criterion—that is, knowing the test scores is of no benefit when predicting the criterion. For the data[3] in Example 1, the value of the validity coefficient is .88, indicating a high degree of validity—higher than is usually found in validity studies of this type. For instance, researchers found a correlation of only .19 for the prediction of job performance

---

[1]The dictionary definition of *empirical* that applies to this discussion is "relying or based on observation rather than theory."

[2]It is also possible to obtain negative coefficients, but they seldom are obtained in validity studies. Negative correlation coefficients are discussed in Topic 47.

[3]The data were created for instructional purposes to illustrate what a strong relationship looks like.

using short-term memory tests.[4]

So how high should predictive validity coefficients be? Of course, higher is better. But how high are they in practice? For an employment test validated against supervisors' ratings, we would be surprised to obtain a coefficient greater than about .60, and we would not be at all surprised to get one as low as .20 or less, indicating poor validity. Why can't we do better? For two reasons. First, success on the job is a complex construct involving many traits such as interpersonal skills (e.g., getting along with coworkers), psychomotor skills (e.g., typing), work habits (e.g., being punctual), etc. It is not reasonable to expect a single test (and especially a paper-and-pencil test) to tap all of these successfully. Second, we do not get higher coefficients because our criteria such as supervisors' ratings are, themselves, less than perfectly reliable and valid. Thus, even if a test were perfectly valid, the coefficient would be less than 1.00 if the supervisors failed to put the employees in the correct order; note that human judgments are subject to biases and other sources of errors.

Sometimes, we determine the empirical validity of a test that is *not* designed to predict future behavior. For example, a new, self-administered version of the Addiction Severity Index (ASI) was validated by correlating scores on it with scores obtained using the expensive and time-consuming original version, which involves a lengthy, structured clinical interview. The original version, which had been widely accepted as being highly valid, was the *criterion* (or "gold standard") by which the new version was judged. In this study, the Drug Domain on the self-administered version of the ASI Drug Domain subscale had a *validity coefficient* of .62, which is moderately high, indicating that to a reasonable extent the less expensive version of the ASI provided information similiar to the more expensive, original version.[5] Another example is to correlate scores on a test that is being validated with scores on a *different test* of the same trait. For instance, scores on the *Beck Depression Inventory* were correlated with scores on the *Revised Hamilton Psychiatric Rating Scale for Depression*, which resulted in a validity coefficient of .71. This relatively strong correlation indicates that to the extent that one of the measures is valid (at a given point in time), the other has a similar degree of validity.[6]

A validity coefficient that is obtained by administering the test and collecting the criterion data at about the same time is called a *concurrent validity coefficient* (as opposed to a *predictive validity coefficient*). The general term for both types of validity examined in this topic is **criterion-related validity**; notice that in both predictive and concurrent validity, we validate by comparing scores with a criterion. The following table shows the relevant features of both.

| Types of Criterion-Related Validity:[1] | What is the **criterion**? | When is the **criterion** measured? |
|---|---|---|
| 1. **Predictive Validity** | A measure of what the test is designed to predict. | After examinees have had a chance to exhibit the predicted behavior. |
| 2. **Concurrent Validity** | An independent measure of the same trait that the test is designed to measure. | At about the same time that the test is administered. |

[1]Both types of criterion-related validity employ the empirical approach; that is, they are based on data that have been collected (planned *empirical* data collection)—not subjective judgments or theory.

---

[4]Source: Verive, J. M. & McDaniel, M. A. (1996). Short-term memory tests in personnel selection: Low adverse impact and high validity. *Intelligence, 23,* 15–32.

[5]Source: Butler, S. F. et al. (2001). Initial validation of a computer-administered Addiction Severity Index: The ASI-MV. *Psychology of Addictive Behaviors, 15,* 4–12.

[6]Source: Beck, A. T., Steer, R. A., & Brown, G. K. (1996). *Manual for the Beck Depression Inventory-Second Edition.* San Antonio: The Psychological Corporation.

# EXERCISE ON TOPIC 25

1. What term do we use for the standard by which a test is being judged?

2. How is *empirical* defined in the topic?

3. What question does predictive validity answer?

4. If a test is perfectly valid, what value will its validity coefficient have?

5. In light of this topic, would you be surprised to get a validity coefficient of .95 for a paper-and-pencil employment test when validated against supervisors' job-performance ratings?

6. If a test has no validity whatsoever, what value will its validity coefficient have?

7. If we collect the criterion data at about the same time the test is being administered, we are examining what type of empirical validity?

## Questions for Discussion

8. Suppose a researcher validated a new multiple-choice reading test by correlating the test scores with teachers' ratings of students' reading abilities (i.e., the scores on the test were correlated with the ratings made by teachers). What is your opinion on using teachers' ratings for this purpose? Could teachers' ratings themselves be less than perfectly valid? Explain.

9. Suppose you wanted to validate a new measure of self-esteem. Name a criterion you might use in a criterion-related validity study. Be prepared to justify its use.

10. The validity of an achievement test might be validated using either content validity (see Topic 24) or concurrent validity (such as correlating the scores with teachers' judgments of students' achievement). Which approach to validity is, in your opinion, more useful for achievement tests? Should both be used? Explain.

## For Students Who Are Planning Research

11. Will you be considering the empirical validity of the instruments you will be using in your research? Explain. (Note that if you use a published instrument, information on empirical validity may already be available in the manual for the instrument.)

# NOTES

The major type of validity that relies heavily on both subjective judgments and empirical data (that is, data based on observations) is **construct validity**.

A *construct* stands for a collection of related behaviors that are associated in a meaningful way. For example, *depression* is a construct that stands for a personality trait that is manifested by behaviors such as lethargy, flat affect when speaking, loss of appetite, loss of sexual drive, preoccupation with suicidal thoughts, difficulty in concentrating on tasks, etc. Notice that each of these is an *indicator* of depression — the construct itself does not have a physical being outside of its indicators. That is, we infer its existence by observing the *collection* of related indicators. The emphasis on *collection* is important because any one sign may be associated with several constructs. For example, although loss of appetite is a sign of depression, it may also be a sign of anxiety, or fear, or falling in love, and so on. Thus, loss of appetite is indicative of depression only when it is found in association with other indicators of depression.

To determine the construct validity of a measuring instrument, we begin by hypothesizing about how the construct that the instrument is designed to measure should affect or relate to other variables. For example, we might hypothesize that students who are very depressed will earn lower grades and be more likely to drop out of college than students who are less depressed. Note that this is a *hypothesis* (see Topic 7) because it *predicts* a relationship between depression and measures of success in college. Also note that we arrived at the hypothesis by making a subjective judgment regarding the likely effects of the indicators of depression on success. If we test the hypothesis using empirical methods, we are conducting a construct validity study.

Let's see how this works for a new 50 question, paper-and-pencil depression *scale*.[1] To determine its construct validity, we could test the hypothesis stated above using a sample of college students as subjects. Let's first suppose that we find *no* relationship between the scores obtained on the depression scale and success in college. What does this mean? Either (1) the scale lacks validity for measuring depression; that is, it measures something else that is not related to success in college, or (2) the hypothesis is wrong. If we continue to hold firmly to our belief in the hypothesis, we will have to conclude that the empirical evidence argues against the validity of the scale.

Next, let's suppose we find a relationship between scores obtained on the new depression scale and success in college. What does this mean? Either (1) the depression scale is, to some degree, valid for measuring depression, or (2) the depression scale measures a variable other than depression that is also related to success in college. This "other variable" could be many things. For instance, maybe the scale is heavily loaded with signs of depression that are also signs of anxiety, so that it is more a measure of anxiety than depression. Because debilitating anxiety may lead to failure in college, the scores on the scale may relate to success in college because it measures anxiety and not depression.

At this point, you should be able to see that determining construct validity is a complex matter —involving both judgment and data. You should also be able to see that it offers only *indirect* evidence regarding the validity of a measure. Notice that direct evidence on the validity of a depression scale could be obtained by determining *criterion-related validity* (see Topic 25). For example, this could be done by correlating scores obtained with the depression scale with clinical psychologists' judgments on how depressed each subject is. This is direct evidence because we are comparing scores from a depression scale with some other established measure of depression—not with an entirely different variable such as success in college.

Since construct validity is complex, let's consider another example. Consider the construct called *dependence on others*. After considering its signs, we might hypothesize that younger children are usually more dependent on adults than older

---

[1]Instruments that measure personality traits are often called *scales* to distinguish them from *tests* of cognitive skills.

children are. If we test the hypothesis and find that the scores on the dependence scale fail to relate to age among children, this result would argue against the validity of the dependence scale. On the other hand, if we find the predicted relationship between the dependence scores and age, this would provide some indirect evidence suggesting that the scale might have some validity.[2]

Because the evidence generated by construct validity studies is indirect, we should be very cautious about declaring a measure to have some validity based on a single study. Instead, we would hope to see a series of construct validity studies for a given measure — testing various hypotheses derived by considering how the construct should be related to other variables — before reaching firm conclusions.

From one perspective, the indirect nature of the evidence obtained in construct validity studies may be regarded as a weakness. However, when there are a series of construct validity studies on a given instrument, we gain insights into how meaningful the scores are in various contexts. This gives a richness to our understanding of how well an instrument works, which is a strength of this approach to validity.

Historically, construct validity has been most closely associated with personality scales. However, its proper application can yield useful information about all types of measures.

It is often desirable to examine a given instrument in several different types of validity studies. The types of validity considered in Topics 24 through 26 are summarized in the following table.

A comparison of major approaches to validity.

| Approaches to Validity | Types | How Determined |
|---|---|---|
| Judgmental | Content | Expert judgments of the appropriateness of the contents. |
| | Face | Judgments based on superficial appearance. |
| Empirical | Predictive | Correlate test scores with criterion scores obtained after examinees have had a chance to perform what is predicted by the test. |
| | Concurrent | Correlate test scores with criterion scores obtained at about the same time. |
| Judgmental-Empirical | Construct | Hypothesize a relationship between the test scores and scores on another variable. Then, test the hypothesis. |

---

[2] As you know from Topic 23, validity is a matter of degree. Thus, the term "*some* validity" is used in this discussion.

# Exercise on Topic 26

1. How is the term *construct* defined in this topic?

2. Is *loss of appetite* a construct?

3. To determine construct validity, we begin by hypothesizing what?

4. Does confirming a hypothesis in a construct validity study offer direct or indirect evidence on the validity of a test?

5. Is the process of determining construct validity purely judgmental?

6. Which two types of validity are classified as "empirical?"

7. Which two types of validity are classified as "judgmental?"

8. Which type of validity is classified as "judgmental-empirical?"

## Questions for Discussion

9. In your opinion, what are some of the physical signs of (or behaviors associated with) the construct we call *industriousness*?

10. To determine the construct validity of a paper-and-pencil industriousness scale, a researcher hypothesized that scores earned on it should be correlated with the number of promotions employees receive on the job. Do you think that this is a good hypothesis for a construct validity study? Explain.

11. Consider the physical signs of *shyness*. Propose a hypothesis on this construct that might be tested in a construct validity study.

## For Students Who Are Planning Research

12. Will you be considering the construct validity of any instruments you will be using in your research? Explain.

# NOTES

# TOPIC 27  RELIABILITY AND ITS RELATIONSHIP TO VALIDITY

A test is said to be **reliable** if it yields *consistent* results. Let's see what this means by considering an extreme example. Suppose your professor writes a midterm exam on research methods that contains only four multiple-choice items. The items are on four different important concepts that were emphasized during instruction; thus, the exam is valid in the sense that it covers appropriate content. Students who have mastered the course content should be concerned about taking such a test because it would be very easy to misinterpret a question or to miss a key term in it and get it wrong — yielding a score of 3 out of 4 right or 75% correct. On the other hand, students who have moved through the semester in a fog, not understanding even basic concepts, should be pleased at the prospect of taking this exam. With only four items, the odds of getting a few right by guessing and, thus, passing the test are reasonably high.

Now let's suppose some students complain about their scores on the midterm, so your professor writes four new multiple-choice items, and again, they are all on appropriate content. After administering the test at the next class meeting (without announcing there would be a second test so students are not motivated to study again), should your professor expect to obtain the same scores as he did the first time? In all likelihood, no. Some students who were lucky in guessing the first time will have their luck wash out. Other students who misinterpreted a key term in a question will not do so on the new set of items. Examining the scores from the two tests provides your professor with information on the *consistency of results* or *reliability*. In this case, he would probably find that the scores are rather *in*consistent from one test to the other.

What can your professor do to increase the reliability of his midterm? Obviously, he can increase the length of the test. This reduces the effects of the occasional ambiguous item *and* the effects of guessing. Finally realizing this principle, your professor (who is a master of the content but a bit dense when it comes to educational measurement) instructs his graduate assistant to come up with a 100-item test overnight. The assistant, being pressed for time, takes the easy route and pulls a standardized test off the shelf. Although it has 100 items, they are on educational psychology, which includes some research concepts but also much material not covered in research methods. Administering this test should give highly reliable results. If we administer it twice, for example, those who don't know the name of the "father of educational psychology" the first time the test is administered won't know his name the second time.[1] Likewise, those who have a good command of educational psychology should do well on both tests. Also, those who don't know the material will have little chance of getting a good grade by guessing on such a large number of items. But, of course, we have a new problem, the test lacks **validity** because it covers the wrong content (see Topics 23 through 26 on validity). This illustrates an important principle: *A test with high reliability may have low validity.*

Here is another example of this principle. An employer wants to reward her best employees with end-of-year bonuses. She decides that to be perfectly fair, she should use a completely objective method for determining who should get the bonuses. To do this, she examines the employees' time cards, and those who were never late for work during the year were selected for bonuses. Notice that this method of measurement is highly reliable — another person could independently perform the same procedure and, if careful, would identify exactly the same employees for bonuses, yielding consistent (reliable) results. But is the procedure valid? Probably only minimally so because the employer's measurement technique is limited to only one characteristic. Those who are outstanding in a number of other ways (such as identifying more effective ways to advertise products) were excluded from the "best" category. Such employees would be justified in complaining that, while the procedure is reliable, it is of very questionable validity.

---

[1]Edward Thorndike of Teachers College (Columbia University) is widely cited as the father of educational psychology primarily because of his influence in promoting the use of empirical methods for studying education.

This brings us to the next principle: When evaluating instruments, *validity is more important than reliability*. This should be clear from considering the example of the employer basing bonuses on employees' time cards. A complex measure involving subjective judgments of employees' performance touching on a variety of important types of behavior and achievement on the job would be much more valid (even if it was only modestly reliable) than a highly reliable measure that considers only punctuality. The latter is likely to lead to cries of unfairness.

Finally, there is a third principle: *To be useful, an instrument must be both reasonably valid and reasonably reliable.*

To understand the complex relationship between reliability and validity, consider Figures A through D.

In Figure A, the gun is aimed in a valid direction (toward the target), and all the shots are consistently directed, indicating that they are reliable.

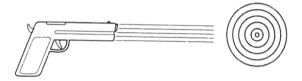

Figure A   Reliable and valid.

In Figure B, the gun is also aimed in the direction of the target, but the shots are widely scattered, indicating low consistency or reliability. The poor reliability makes it unlikely we will hit the target; thus, poor reliability undermines our attempt to achieve validity.

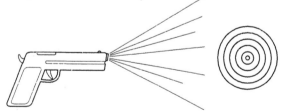

Figure B   Unreliable, which undermines the valid aim of the gun. Not useful.

In Figure C, the gun is not pointed at the target, making it invalid, but there is great consistency in the shots, indicating that it is reliable. (In a sense, it is reliably invalid.)

Figure C   Reliable but invalid. Not useful.

In Figure D, the gun is not pointed at the target, making it invalid, and the lack of consistency in the direction of the shots indicates its poor reliability.

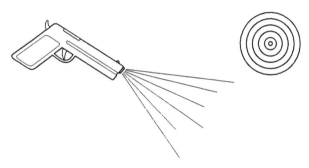

Figure D   Unreliable and invalid. Not useful.

Of course, Figure A represents the ideal in measurement. For most measures in the social and behavioral sciences, however, we should expect the direction of the gun to be off at least a small amount, indicating less than perfect validity; we should also expect some scatter in the shots, indicating less than perfect reliability.[2] Clearly, our first priority should be to point the gun in the correct *general direction*, which promotes validity. Then we should work on increasing reliability.

---

[2]Examination of the technical manuals for published tests indicates that test makers tend to be more successful in achieving high reliability than in achieving high validity.

# EXERCISE ON TOPIC 27

1. A test is said to be reliable if it yields what?

2. Would you expect a very short multiple-choice test to be highly reliable?

3. Is it possible for a test with high reliability to have low validity?

4. Overall, is validity or reliability more important when evaluating an instrument?

5. If a test is highly reliable but highly invalid, is it useful?

6. In light of the topic, should you expect most instruments to be both perfectly reliable and valid?

## Questions for Discussion

7. Consider the example in the topic of the employer who was trying to identify the "best" employees using a measure of punctuality because it was reliable even though it was not especially valid. Name one or two other traits that might be examined in evaluating employees. Comment on whether you think each of your suggestions can be measured reliably. Also, comment on whether you think each is more valid than punctuality for the purpose described in the topic.

8. Suppose you were offered a choice between two midterm exams for your research methods class. The first one contains eight short essay questions, and the second contains 38 multiple-choice questions. Both are on appropriate content. Which would you prefer to take? Why? In your opinion, which one is likely to be more reliable?

## For Students Who Are Planning Research

9. Will you be considering the reliability of any instruments you will be using in your research? Explain. (Note that reliability will be considered in more detail in the next topic.)

# NOTES

# TOPIC 28  MEASURES OF RELIABILITY

How can we determine reliability? The classic model is to measure twice and then check to see if the two sets of measurements are consistent with each other.

First, let's consider **interobserver reliability**. Suppose we want to test the hypothesis that tall people are waited on more quickly in retail stores than short people. To do this, we could observe unobtrusively[1] to (1) classify customers as either tall, medium, or short, and (2) count the number of seconds from the time each customer enters the store to the time a salesperson speaks to him or her.

Since judgments of height might not be reliable, we could check on it by having two observers independently observe to assess it. We could then determine the *percentage* of subjects who were put in the same height category (tall, medium, or short) by *both observers*. How high should the percentage be? Although there is no standard answer to this question, it's clear that if the percentage gets too low (say, less than 60% agreement), we have a serious problem — either one or both of the observers is not a good judge of height. Such a lack of consistency in their judgments would doom the entire study.

Our measure of the number of seconds also might be unreliable if, for example, the observers are easily distracted by other events, are inattentive to the measurement task, and so on. To check on this possibility, we could compare the measurements reported by the two observers. When there are two quantitative scores per subject (such as the number of seconds for each customer as indicated by each observer), we can check on the degree of relationship by computing a correlation coefficient.[2] As you may recall from our discussion of empirical validity (see Topic 25), a correlation coefficient may vary in value from 0.00 to 1.00.[3] A 1.00 indicates perfect reliability — that is, the rank order of the customers based on the observations by one observer is the same as the

rank order based on the observations made by the other observer. When we use *correlation coefficients* to describe reliability, we call them *reliability coefficients*. When we use them to describe the agreement between observers, they are usually called *interobserver reliability coefficients*.

Notice that when studying interobserver reliability, we usually obtain the two measurements *at the same time* (that is, the two observers observe the same subjects at the same time). In contrast, in **test-retest reliability**, we measure at *two different points in time*. For example, suppose we want to know the reliability of a new test designed to assess the ability to learn college-level math. We might administer the test one week and then readminister it two weeks later. Since the ability to learn college-level math should not change very much from week to week, we should expect consistent scores if the test is reliable. Once again, for two sets of scores, we would compute a correlation coefficient, which would indicate the *test-retest reliability* of the test.

Some published tests come in two parallel (or equivalent) forms that are designed to be interchangeable with each other; they have different items that cover the same content. When they are available, **parallel-forms reliability** should be determined. This is usually done by administering one form of the test to examinees and, about a week later, administering the other form to the same examinees—yielding two scores per person. When the sets of scores are correlated, the result indicates the *parallel-forms reliability* of the test.

How high should a reliability coefficient be? Most published tests have reliability coefficients of .80 or higher—so we should strive to select or build instruments that have coefficients this high, especially if we plan to interpret the scores for *individuals*. For *group averages* based on groups of subjects of about 25 or more, instruments with reliability coefficients as low as .50 can be serviceable. To understand why we can tolerate

---

[1]We attempt to measure unobtrusively to avoid changing subjects' behavior. For example, if salespeople know that we are observing them, they might modify their normal behavior toward customers.

[2]See Topic 47 of this book for a detailed discussion of correlation.

[3]Correlation coefficients may also be negative, as discussed in Topic 47. In the unlikely event that you get a negative when studying reliability, think of it as representing no reliability.

rather low reliability coefficients in research in which we are examining averages, first keep in mind that reliability coefficients indicate the reliability of *individuals' scores*. Theory tells us that averages are more reliable than the scores that underlie them because when computing an average, the negative errors tend to cancel out the positive errors. For instance, suppose we want to compare the average age of parents who read extensively with their sixth-grade children with the average age of parents who do not. Asking children their parents' ages is likely to be unreliable. However, we should expect about half the children to overestimate the ages and half to underestimate them; to the extent that this is true, the averages may be reasonably accurate since the underestimates will cancel the overestimates.

At this point you might examine Appendix E, which contains a discussion of other methods of examining reliability.

# EXERCISE ON TOPIC 28

1. We need at least how many observers to determine interobserver reliability?

2. When there are two quantitative scores per subject, we can compute what statistic to describe reliability?

3. Do we usually measure at two different points in time to estimate interobserver reliability?

4. Do we usually measure at two different points in time to estimate test-retest reliability?

5. According to this topic, most published tests have reliability coefficients that are about how high?

6. According to the topic, serviceable reliability coefficients may be how low if we are measuring in order to examine group averages?

## Questions for Discussion

7. In your opinion, which of the following variables mentioned in the topic would probably be easier to measure reliably? (1) height of customers based on observations made from a distance *or* (2) number of seconds from the time customers enter a store until a salesperson greets them, also based on observations from a distance. Explain your choice.

8. For measures of which of the following variables would test-retest reliability (with the instruments administered two weeks apart) probably be more appropriate? (1) voters' opinion on the honesty of two presidential candidates *or* (2) racial prejudice against Asian-Americans. Explain your choice.

## For Students Who Are Planning Research

9. Will you be considering the reliability of any instruments you will be using in your research? If so, which method(s) for examining reliability will you use? Explain.

# TOPIC 29  NORM- AND CRITERION-REFERENCED TESTS

Tests designed to facilitate a comparison of an individual's performance with that of a norm group are called **norm-referenced tests (NRT)**.[1] For example, if you take a test and are told that your *percentile rank* is 64, you know that you scored higher[2] than 64% of those in the norm group. Often the norm group is a national sample of examinees, but it may also be either a local population (such as all seniors in a school district) or a sample of a local population (such as a random sample of all seniors in a state).

Tests designed to measure the extent to which individual examinees have met performance standards are called **criterion-referenced tests (CRT)**.[3] For instance, suppose we wish to test student nurses on their ability to give an injection. We might draw up a list of ten behaviors that must be performed correctly for a student to pass the test—such as measuring the correct amount of medication, using a sterile needle, and so on. In this case, performing all of the behaviors correctly is the criterion (that is, performance standard).[4] Notice that the interpretation of an examinee's test score is independent of how other students perform; for example, you might be the best in a group with 9 items right, but you, along with everyone else, has failed. Being higher or lower than others who take the same criterion-referenced test is irrelevant to the interpretation.

Those who build norm-referenced tests approach the task differently than those who build criterion-referenced tests. NRTs are intentionally built to be of medium difficulty—specifically, items that are passed by only about 50% of the examinees in tryouts are favored in the selection of items for the final versions of the tests. It is essential that an NRT be somewhat difficult (but not too difficult) because it facilitates the comparison of an individual with a group. This can be seen most easily at the extremes. For example, if we foolishly built an NRT that was so easy that all subjects in the norm group got every item right, we could not interpret scores in terms of who has a higher or lower score than other examinees since everyone has the same score. The same problem would occur if we built an NRT that was so difficult that all the examinees got all of the items wrong.

In contrast, when building a CRT, item difficulty is of little concern. Expert judgment is used to determine the desired level of performance and how to test for it—these judgments are influenced very little by how "difficult" a task is. Certainly, this approach is often appropriate. For instance, would you want the professors at a nursing school to drop the item on measuring the correct amount of medication before injecting it simply because it's too difficult for their students? Of course not; we'd want them to include the item regardless of its difficulty level.

The need to have items of modest difficulty in NRTs is the basis of a major criticism of this type of test. Specifically, the criticism is that building NRTs is primarily driven by statistical considerations (that is, item difficulty) and not by content considerations. Of course, those who build NRTs have to consider carefully the content that a test should cover, but essential content may be deleted if the items that measure it are very easy or very difficult in try-outs of the items.

---

[1]Some people refer to *norm-referenced tests* as *standardized tests*. However, it is better to reserve the term *standardized* to describe tests that come with standard directions for administration and interpretation. Both *norm-referenced tests* and *criterion-referenced tests* may be standardized.

[2]Strictly speaking, a percentile rank indicates the percentage that an examinee scored *as high as or higher than*.

[3]You may recall that the term *criterion-related* validity was used in Topic 25. Note that the word *criterion* is being used in both contexts to mean *a standard*. In Topic 25, we discussed using a standard for validating tests; here we are discussing using a standard to interpret the scores of individuals. These are, of course, separate matters, even though we use the same adjective.

[4]Performance standards are established by expert judgment and may be less than 100% correct, depending on the trait being measured. For example, on a typing test, we might require only 95% accuracy. Of course, performance standards are not always expressed as a percentage. We can use descriptive labels such as "expert," "novice," etc.

Which type of test should be favored in research? The answer depends on the research purpose. Here are two general rules:

1. If our purpose is to describe specifically what examinees know and can do, criterion-referenced tests should be considered.

    Example: To what extent can voters understand ballot propositions?

    Example: Have students mastered the essentials of simple addition?

2. If we want to examine how a local group differs from a larger norm group, norm-referenced tests should be considered.[5]

    Example: How well are students in New York doing in reading in comparison with the national average?

# EXERCISE ON TOPIC 29

1. A norm-referenced test is designed to facilitate a comparison of an individual's performance with what?

2. What is the definition of a criterion-referenced test?

3. In which type of test are items that are passed by about 50% of the subjects favored in item selection?

4. In which type of test are items selected based on the content they cover without regard to item difficulty?

5. Which type of test should be considered for use in research where the purpose is to describe specifically what examinees can and cannot do?

## Questions for Discussion

6. Assume you are a parent and your child's second-grade teacher offers to provide you with *either* scores on a norm-referenced test *or* a criterion-referenced test of your child's basic math ability. Which would you choose? Why?

7. If you were conducting research on the percentage of students whose swimming skills are good enough to save themselves if they jump into the deep end of a pool, would you choose a norm-referenced test or criterion-referenced test? Why?

## For Students Who Are Planning Research

8. Will you be using norm-referenced tests? Criterion-referenced tests? Explain the basis for your choice.

---

[5]To make predictions, we need tests that differentiate among subjects. Since norm-referenced tests are specifically built to make differentiations by being of medium difficulty, they are also useful in prediction studies.

When we measure achievement, aptitude, and intelligence, we want examinees to show us their best—to perform at their optimum.

An **achievement test** measures *knowledge and skills people have acquired*. When we conduct research on the effectiveness of direct, planned instruction, we should use achievement tests designed to measure the objectives of that instruction. To the extent that the tests do that, they are *valid* (that is, they measure what they should).

Multiple-choice tests of achievement are popular with researchers because of the ease with which they can be administered and scored. Indeed, they are often appropriate when we want a quick snapshot of subjects' achievement. We can also measure achievement by having subjects write answers to open-ended questions (such as essay questions), by evaluating subjects' performance (such as a musical performance) or by assessing products (such as a portfolio of watercolor paintings). Scoring of the latter types is more time-consuming than scoring multiple-choice tests and may be *unreliable* unless we make sure that the scorers know specifically what characteristics of the essays, products, or performances they are to consider and how much weight to give to each characteristic in arriving at the scores. For example, to evaluate the ability of a student nurse to give an injection, we could develop a list of desirable characteristics such as "measures the appropriate amount of medication," "checks the patient's armband," etc. These can be the basis for a *checklist* (a list of desirable characteristics of a product or performance, for each of which a point is awarded) or a *rating scale* (for example, "excellent, above average, average, below average, poor" that are applied in evaluating each characteristic).

An **aptitude test** is designed to *predict some specific type of achievement*. An example is the College Board's *Scholastic Aptitude Test* (*SAT*), which is designed to predict success in college. The validity of an aptitude test is determined by correlating the scores subjects earn (such as *SAT* scores determined while subjects are in high school) with a measure of achievement obtained at a later date (such as freshman GPA in college). Other widely used aptitude tests are reading readiness tests (designed to predict reading achievement in the first grade by measuring whether examinees can discriminate among shapes, have basic concepts such as color names, etc.) and algebra prognosis tests (designed to predict achievement in algebra by measuring basic math skills that are used in algebra). Most aptitude tests are developed by commercial test publishers. Typically, they have low to modest validity (with validity coefficients of about .30 to .60) and high reliability (with reliability coefficients of .85 or higher).

An **intelligence test** is designed to *predict achievement in general*—not any one specific type. The most popular intelligence tests are (1) culturally loaded and (2) measure knowledge and skills that can be acquired with instruction (with questions such as, "How far is it from New York to Los Angeles?"). The arguable assumption underlying them is that all people are exposed to such information and the more intelligent people are more likely to retain it. Most modern psychologists, however, reject the notion that such tests measure innate (inborn) intelligence. At best, they represent one type of intelligence that has been acquired in some specific cultural milieu. Commercially available intelligence tests of this type have very low to modest validity for predicting achievement in school—a degree of validity that can be achieved with less controversial aptitude tests.

Efforts have been made to develop culture-free intelligence tests. Typical efforts in this area have concentrated on nonverbal tasks because of the high cultural load of language usage. These tests usually are less predictive of subsequent achievement than the more traditional intelligence tests, possibly because achievement is accomplished in a cultural context.

Research on intelligence can be controversial when, for example, researchers assume that intelligence tests measure innate ability or measure all important aspects of intelligence. Issues such as racial differences in innate intelligence, if worthy of investigation at all, cannot be satisfactorily

investigated with the instruments available at this
time.

# Exercise on Topic 30

1. Which type of test is designed to predict achievement in general?

2. An algebra prognosis test is an example of what type of test?

3. A test designed to measure how much students learn in a research methods course is what type of test?

4. A test designed to predict success in learning how to become a telephone operator is what type of test?

5. A list of desirable characteristics of a product or performance is known as what?

6. How can we increase the reliability of scoring essays, products, and performances?

7. According to the topic, are intelligence tests good measures of innate ability?

8. According to the topic, how valid are commercially published aptitude tests?

## Questions for Discussion

9. Did you ever take an achievement test on which you did not perform up to your optimum? If yes, briefly describe why. Was the test maker or test administrator responsible for your less than optimum performance?

10. Do you think that research on racial differences in intelligence is worth pursuing? Why? Why not?

11. Name a specific type of achievement for which you think that scores obtained by using a checklist or rating scale would be more valid than scores obtained by using a multiple-choice test.

## For Students Who Are Planning Research

12. Will you be using an achievement test? Have you selected it yet? Explain.

13. Will you be using an aptitude test? What will it be designed to predict? Explain.

14. Will you be using an intelligence test? Will it be one designed to be "culture-free?" If yes, do you believe it is really culture-free? Explain.

# TOPIC 31  MEASURES OF TYPICAL PERFORMANCE

As you know from the last topic, when we measure achievement, aptitude, and intelligence, we encourage subjects to show us their best. When we measure personality traits such as attitudes, interests, dispositions, as well as deep-seated personality traits, we want to determine subjects' *typical* level of performance. For example, when selecting employees to work as salespeople, we might want to know how assertive each applicant typically is—not just how assertive they claim to be during an interview or in their responses to an assertiveness scale (a series of questions that are scored to get an overall assertiveness score). Our concern here is that the applicants might indicate what is *socially desirable* rather than indicate their true level of assertiveness in order to increase their chances of employment.

People often are hesitant to reveal that they have socially *undesirable* traits even when they have nothing directly to gain by being deceitful. Thus, the responses of subjects in research projects may be influenced by social desirability. To the extent that we can reduce social desirability, we increase the validity of personality measures.

There are three basic approaches to reducing social desirability in subjects' responses. First, by administering personality measures anonymously, we may reduce this tendency.

Another approach to reducing the effects of social desirability is to observe behavior unobtrusively (without the subjects' awareness—to the extent this is ethically possible) and rate selected characteristics such as aggressiveness.

A third approach is to use *projective techniques*. These provide loosely structured or ambiguous stimuli such as ink blots. As subjects respond to these stimuli, such as by telling what they see, they are presumed to be projecting their feelings and beliefs and revealing them in their responses. For instance, we might infer that subjects whose responses to ink blots contain numerous references to aggressiveness are themselves aggressive. To the extent that subjects are unaware of the specific traits an investigator is looking for, the tendency to give socially desirable responses is reduced. The literature on popular projective techniques is quite mixed in the assessments of their validity and reliability—with some studies showing that they are remarkably deficient in these respects. Thus, they are best used only by those who have had formal training in their administration and scoring.

The development of valid and reliable measures of personality traits is complex and difficult and, for many traits, is best left to experts in personality measurement.

Researchers who want to measure attitudes usually have success by developing Likert-type scales, with choices ranging from "Strongly agree" to "Strongly disagree." Each item should present a clear statement on a single topic. For instance, to measure attitudes toward school, we might use statements such as, "In the mornings, I look forward to going to school" and "I get along well with my teacher." To reduce response bias (such as marking strongly agree to all items without considering the individual items), it's a good idea to provide some positive and some negative statements.

Of course, the statements should be derived from an analysis of the possible components of the attitude. For attitude toward school, we might have several statements in each of these areas: (a) learning in academic areas, (b) relationships with classmates, (c) relationships with teachers and staff, (d) participation in extracurricular activities, and so on. Such an analysis helps to assure that the attitude scale is comprehensive, contributing to its validity. To reduce social desirability and obtain an indication of the typical attitude toward school, such instruments should be administered anonymously, if possible.

Subjects' responses to questionnaire items that solicit factual information—especially about sensitive topics such as income and sexual practices—may also be influenced by social desirability. Once again, anonymity of responses may reduce its effects.

# Exercise on Topic 31

1. Do we usually want subjects to show us their best when we measure personality traits?

2. In this topic, what is the main reason for administering personality measures anonymously?

3. What do we reduce by observing behavior unobtrusively?

4. Loosely structured stimuli are used in which type of personality measure?

5. According to this topic, which type of personality measure should be used only by those who have formal training in their use?

6. What are the choices in a Likert-type scale?

7. The Likert-type scale is recommended for measuring which type of trait?

8. According to this topic, can responses to questionnaire items that solicit factual information be influenced by social desirability?

## Questions for Discussion

9. Have you ever given a socially desirable response when it was not true of you when being interviewed or answering a questionnaire? If yes, briefly describe why. Is there anything the interviewer or questionnaire writer could have done to make you comfortable in being more forthright?

10. Write three statements that could be used with a Likert-type scale to measure attitudes toward your research methods class. Each should be on a different aspect of the class such as the textbook, the instructor, etc.

## For Students Who Are Planning Research

11. Will you be using a measure of typical performance? If so, to what extent might it be subject to the influence of social desirability? Explain.

12. Will you be measuring attitudes? If yes, will you use a Likert-type scale? Explain.

# PART E

# EXPERIMENTAL DESIGN

As you know from Part A, researchers give treatments in experiments in order to observe their effects on subjects' behavior. In this section, we will examine various designs for experiments. Specifically, we will look at designs for true experiments, quasi-experiments, and pre-experiments. We will also consider the external validity of experiments (which answers the question, "Can we generalize beyond the experimental setting?") as well as their internal validity (which answers the question, "Did the treatments, in fact, cause the observed differences?")[1]

---

[1]This part highlights some of the main ideas in Campbell, D. T. & Stanley, J. C. (1963). *Experimental and quasi-experimental designs for research*. Chicago: Rand McNally.

# NOTES

As you know from earlier topics, the purpose of an experiment is to explore cause and effect relationships. In this discussion, we will use terminology and symbols first suggested by Campbell and Stanley.[1]

First, let's examine a classic design for exploring cause and effect relationships:

**Design 1:**

| Assign subjects at random to groups. | Group A: (Experimental Group) | Pretest | Experimental Treatment | Posttest |
| --- | --- | --- | --- | --- |
| | Group B: (Control Group) | Pretest | Control Condition | Posttest |

Design 1 is a **pretest-posttest randomized control group design**. By assigning subjects at random to groups, we are assured that there are no biases in the assignment.[2] That is, the two groups of subjects are equal except for random differences.

If we find that the experimental group makes greater gains from pretest to posttest than the control group in Design 1 *and* if we have treated the two groups the same in all respects except for the experimental treatment, we can attribute the difference to only one of two causes: (1) the treatment or (2) random errors. As you will see in Part F of this book, we can use inferential statistics to assess the role of random errors in creating any differences we observe; thus, we can tolerate random errors because we can interpret the results in light of their possible effects. There are no generalizable statistical techniques for assessing the influence of bias; hence, we strive to avoid bias in assignment.

We can simplify the representation of Design 1 by using symbols suggested by Campbell and Stanley: R (stands for random assignment to groups), O (stands for observation or measurement, whether pretest or posttest), and X (stands for experimental treatment). There is no symbol for control condition, so it is represented by a blank. Note that a control condition may include some type of treatment (in education, it might be a traditional form of instruction; in medicine, it might be a placebo—a sugar pill). Thus, the control condition is the standard by which we will judge the effectiveness of the experimental treatment. Using symbols, Design 1 looks like this:

$$R \; O \; X \; O$$
$$R \; O \quad\;\; O$$

The advantage of the pretest is that we can determine how much each group has *gained*—not just whether they are different at the end of the experiment. However, sometimes having a pretest is a disadvantage since it can sensitize subjects to the experimental treatment and, in effect, become part of the treatment. For example, by taking a pretest at the beginning of an experimental course of instruction, subjects can gain an overview of what will be covered, in how much depth the material will be covered, etc. Thus, changes we observe in the experimental group may be the result of a *combination of the pretest and the treatment*. This problem is called *pretest sensitization* (also called the *reactive effect of testing*). It can be overcome by conducting an experiment without a pretest, as is shown in Design 2, which is a **posttest-only randomized control group design**.

**Design 2:**

$$R \; X \; O$$
$$R \quad\;\; O$$

At first, the lack of a pretest may seem to be a flaw, but remember that the comparability of the two groups in Design 1 was achieved by assigning subjects at random to the two groups. This initial comparability is also achieved in Design 2 by this process. In other words, it is not the pretest that makes the two groups comparable; it is the random assignment.

We can have the best of both worlds by using the **Solomon randomized four-group design,**

---

[1]Campbell, D. T. & Stanley, J. C. (1963). *Experimental and quasi-experimental designs for research*. Chicago: Rand McNally.
[2]See Topic 18 for a discussion of how to select subjects at random. If we select half of them at random to be the experimental group and make the rest the control group, we have used random assignment to groups.

which is just a combination of Designs 1 and 2; it is shown here as Design 3:

**Design 3:**

```
R O X O
R O   O
R   X O
R     O
```

The advantage of Design 3 is that we can compare the first two groups to determine how much gain is made, and we can also compare the last two groups to determine whether the treatment is more effective than the control condition in the absence of a pretest (without pretest sensitization). The only potential drawback to Design 3 is that you must have a reasonably large pool of subjects to begin with so that when they are divided into four groups, each of the groups will have a sufficient number to yield reliable results. How many is enough? The answer is complex, but generally speaking, it probably would be unwise to use the four-group design instead of a two-group design if you have a total pool of fewer than 48 subjects.

All three of the above designs are called **true designs** because they are strong in terms of their *internal validity*—a topic that is taken up next. True designs are easy to spot because they all involve random assignment to treatments.

# EXERCISE ON TOPIC 32

1. What is the purpose of an experiment?

2. How can we ensure that there are no biases in the assignment of subjects to groups in an experiment?

3. In a diagram for an experimental design, the symbol "O" stands for what?

4. In a diagram for an experimental design, the symbol "X" stands for what?

5. What is the name of the potential problem caused by the pretest in the pretest-posttest randomized control group design?

6. What is the name of the true experimental design that has no pretests?

7. What is a potential drawback to the Solomon randomized four-group design?

8. How are subjects assigned to groups in all true experiments?

## Question for Discussion

9. Briefly describe an experimental problem for which you probably would not be able to assign subjects at random to conditions.

## For Students Who Are Planning Research

10. Will you be conducting an experiment? If so, will you be using a true experimental design? Explain.

# TOPIC 33 THREATS TO INTERNAL VALIDITY

Suppose that we observe significant changes in subjects' behavior in an experiment. Can we attribute these changes to the effects of the treatment(s)? Depending on the design of the experiment, there may be explanations for the changes other than the treatment; these are called **threats to internal validity**. It is easiest to understand these in the context of a poor experiment—specifically, one in which we pretest, treat, and then posttest one group of subjects—with no control group. Using the symbols described in the previous topic, the design looks like this:

O X O

Suppose the treatment (X) was designed to increase subjects' self-concept, and we observe an average gain of 9 points in self-concept from pretest (the first O) to posttest (the second O). Indeed, the treatment could be responsible for the increase. Another possibility is the internal threat called **history** (other environmental influences on the subjects between the pretest and posttest). For example, perhaps some of the subjects read a new self-help book that improved their self-concepts during the same period of time that the treatment was being administered. Thus, the gain could have resulted from reading the book and not from the treatment.

Another threat in this design is **maturation**. Perhaps the subjects matured during the period between the pretest and posttest, and the increase is due to maturation and not the treatment.

**Instrumentation** is another threat. This refers to possible changes in the instrument (measurement procedure) from the time it was used as a pretest to the time it was used as the posttest. For example, the particular individuals used to make the pretest observations may have been less astute at noticing signs of a good self-concept than the individuals who made the posttest observations.

Another threat is **testing**—the effects of the pretest on the performance on the posttest. For example, while taking the pretest self-concept scale, students may have learned how to interpret the questions. Their posttest performance might be affected by this learning experience.

**Statistical regression** is another threat if the subjects were selected on the basis of their extreme scores. For example, perhaps a large group of students were tested for self-concept, and those in the lowest 20% were selected for treatment in our experiment. A principle of measurement is that those who are extremely low on a screening test will, on the average, probably have a higher score when tested again, purely because of the nature of random errors created by the less than perfect reliability of the measures we use.[1]

The next threat to internal validity can be seen when we have two comparison groups that are *not* formed at random. Suppose, for example, we use the students in one school as the experimental group and those in another as a control. Since students are not assigned to schools at random, we are using intact (previously existing) groups. We diagram this by putting a dashed line between the groups as shown here:

O X O
-----------
O     O

Notice that when we do not assign subjects to the two groups at random, there is the strong possibility that the two groups are not initially the same in all important respects, which is the threat called **selection**. Selection can *interact* with all of the other threats to internal validity. For example, consider **selection-history interaction**. Because the selection of subjects for the two groups was not at random, they may be systematically subjected to different experiences—for example, maybe the teachers in the school with the experimental group took a self-concept workshop (that was not part of the treatment) and applied what they learned to their students. Thus, the improvement in self-concepts may be the result of the teachers' efforts and not of the treatment. Another

---

[1]Statistical regression is hard to grasp unless you have a good background in measurement theory. However, you may recall from your study of other sciences the principle of "regression toward the mean." Those who are very low will, on the average, tend to be higher on retesting (closer to the mean—an average), and those who are very high will tend to be lower on retesting.

example is **selection-maturation interaction**. Perhaps the two groups, on the average, are at somewhat different developmental stages, which leads to different rates of development in the two groups, which could affect self-concept.

Selection can also interact with a threat called **mortality** (differential loss of subjects from the groups to be compared). For instance, those in an experimental school may have a higher drop-out rate than those in a control school. To the extent that changes in self-concept are related to dropping out, the greater loss of subjects may affect the comparison of the two groups.

All threats to internal validity can be overcome by using a **true experimental design** (see Topic 32), in which subjects are assigned at random to experimental and control conditions. Because random assignment has no bias (or favorites), both groups are equally likely to experience the same environmental events (have the same history), are equally likely to mature at the same rates, and so on. In the next topic, we will examine threats to *external validity*.

# EXERCISE ON TOPIC 33

1. What is the name of the threat that says taking a pretest may affect performance on a posttest?

2. Suppose that while an experimental group is being taught letters of the alphabet in school as a treatment, the students in the group are watching *Sesame Street* and learning the names of the letters. What is the name of the threat that this illustrates?

3. If observers are more tired and less astute when making posttest observations than when making pretest observations, what threat is operating?

4. What is the name of the threat posed by nonrandom assignment of subjects to experimental and control groups?

5. If infants naturally improve in visual acuity and, thus, perform better at the end of an experiment than at the beginning, what threat is operating?

6. Under what circumstance will statistical regression operate?

7. How can we overcome all of the threats to internal validity?

## Question for Discussion

8. Suppose a researcher gave a series of healthy-behavior workshops over a period of six months, and then determined that five of the employees had quit smoking during the six-month period. His interpretation was that the workshops caused the decrease in smoking. Is his interpretation flawed? Explain.

## For Students Who Are Planning Research

9. If you will be conducting an experiment, which threats, if any, will it be subject to? Explain.

# Topic 34  Threats to External Validity

Suppose that we observe significant changes in subjects' behavior in an experiment. Can we generalize with confidence (1) to the larger population from which the subjects were drawn and (2) to the natural setting in which the larger population conducts its everyday activities? The answer depends on the extent to which the experiment is subject to **threats to external validity**.

The first threat is **selection bias** and its interaction with the experimental (independent) variable. You probably recall from Part C of this book that if a sample is biased, our ability to generalize to a population is greatly limited—in a very strict scientific sense, no generalizations should be made. This threat reminds us that if a biased sample of subjects is used in an experiment (such as the students who happen to be in one professor's class), we will not know whether the effects of the treatment (observed in that class) can be expected if the treatment is administered to the entire population. Of course, the way to control this threat is to select the subjects for an experiment at random from a population; a random sample is, by definition, unbiased.

Another threat is the **reactive effects of experimental arrangements**. This threat reminds us that if the experimental setting is different from the natural setting in which the population usually operates, the effects we observe in the experimental setting may not generalize to the natural setting. For example, if the treatment is administered in a lab on a college campus, the responsiveness of the subjects may be different from the responsiveness of the population in public school classrooms. Thus, it may be risky to generalize from an experimental setting to a natural setting. The way to control this threat is to conduct experiments under natural conditions, when possible.

The possible **reactive effect of testing** (also called *pretest sensitization*) is another threat. This means that the pretest might influence how the subjects respond to the experimental treatment. For example, if we give a pretest on racial prejudice and then administer a treatment designed to lessen prejudice, how subjects respond to the treatment may be affected by the experience of taking the pretest. For example, having to think about prejudice (while taking the pretest) might change subjects' sensitivity to the treatment. This

becomes a problem if we want to generalize about how the treatment will work in the population *if* the population will not be given a pretest. This threat was mentioned in Topic 32 where it was pointed out that we can conduct true experiments without pretests, thereby eliminating this threat.

**Multiple-treatment interference** is a threat when the same subjects are given more than one treatment. For example, we might give subjects no praise at first for correct answers, then start giving them moderate amounts of praise, and finally give them large amounts of praise. Suppose we find that large amounts of praise works best. Will it work in the same way in the population? Our generalization will be risky if those in the population will not first be given the no praise condition, then the moderate praise condition, and finally the large amounts of praise. In other words, the first two conditions (no praise and moderate praise) may make the sample of subjects no longer representative of the population that is not subjected to these conditions.

Let's review the distinction between **internal validity** (see Topic 33) and **external validity**. As you know from this topic, the external validity of an experiment is concerned with, "To whom and under what circumstances can the results be generalized?" Internal validity is concerned with the question, "Is the treatment, *in this particular case*, responsible for the observed change(s)?" Thus, threats to internal validity are potential explanations for the observed changes; that is, they become *confounded* with the treatment as an explanation. Threats to internal validity are controlled by using *true experimental* designs (see Topic 32). Note that even if an experiment has excellent internal validity, it may not be appropriate to generalize the results to other population(s) because of the threats to external validity discussed in this topic.

In the next two topics, we will consider other types of designs—specifically pre-experimental and quasi-experimental designs.

# Exercise on Topic 34

1. Which type of validity deals with the question of whether we can generalize with confidence to a larger population in a natural setting?

2. Which type of validity deals with whether the treatment is responsible for the changes observed in the experimental setting?

3. What is the name of the threat that warns us to be careful in generalizing the results to a population when an experiment is conducted on a nonrandom sample?

4. Suppose a random sample of workers in a factory is exposed to five different reward systems, with each system being used for one month. What is the name of the threat that reminds us that the results may not generalize to the population of workers if the population is to be exposed to only the last reward system tried in the experiment?

5. Suppose the experimental classroom has research observers present at all times. What is the name of the threat that reminds us that the result may not generalize to other classrooms without observers?

6. If a pretest causes subjects to be more or less sensitive to a treatment, what threat is operating?

## Question for Discussion

7. Briefly describe an experiment that has high internal validity but low external validity.

## For Students Who Are Planning Research

8. If you will be conducting an experiment, which threats to external validity, if any, will it be subject to? Explain.

# TOPIC 35 PRE-EXPERIMENTAL DESIGNS

The three designs we will examine in this topic are of very little value for investigating cause-and-effect relationships because of their poor internal validity. Thus, they are called **pre-experimental designs**.

We have already seen one of them, the **one-group pretest-posttest design**, in Topic 33, where its weaknesses were explored. Its diagram is shown here as Design 4.[1]

**Design 4:**

O X O

You may recall from Topic 33 that changes from pretest to posttest in Design 4 may be attributable to *history, maturation, instrumentation, testing,* and, if the subjects were selected on the basis of extreme scores, *statistical regression*[2] (see Topic 33 for a discussion of these threats to internal validity) — in addition to the possible effects of the treatment. Thus, the interpretation of change is *confounded* by multiple explanations.

Design 5 is called the **one-shot case study**. In it, one group is given a treatment (X) followed by a test (O). This is its diagram:

**Design 5:**

X O

An example of Design 5 is when a teacher provides instruction on a unit and follows it with a test. For instructional purposes, there is nothing wrong with the design. However, if we want to know whether the instruction *caused* whatever achievement we see on the test, the design is useless because there is no comparison of observations. We do not know whether the students achieved anything as a result of the course without a pretest (or randomly selected control group); that is, for all we know the achievement they display on the posttest is at the same level they might have displayed on a pretest, if it was given.[3]

Design 6, the **static-group comparison design**, has two groups, but subjects are not assigned to the groups at random. The dashed line between the two groups indicates that they are intact (previously existing groups).

**Design 6:**

X O
.............
O

The obvious problem with Design 6 is the threat to internal validity called *selection* (the selection of the two groups was not made in such a way that we can have confidence that they are initially the same in all important respects).[4] If we have no basis for knowing that they were the same at the beginning of the experiment, we cannot interpret the differences to assess the effects of the treatment. For all we know, the experimental group was superior to the control group to begin with.[5]

We have examined the three pre-experimental designs in order to warn against their use in studies designed to explore cause-and-effect relationships. However, they sometimes are useful in *preliminary pilot studies* in which our goal is to try out potential treatments and measuring tools to learn more about the acceptability and accuracy of them—not to ferret out causal relationships. For example, we might administer a

---

[1]Each of the designs in this part are given a number for reference in class discussions. The numbering system is not a universal one; thus, in discussions outside of class, refer to the names of the designs given in bold-faced type — not to the design numbers.

[2]Campbell and Stanley (1963) note that this design is also subject to the *interaction of selection with history, maturation,* etc. See Campbell, D. T. & Stanley, J. C. (1963). *Experimental and quasi-experimental designs for research.* Chicago: Rand McNally.

[3]Campbell and Stanley (1993) note that this design is subject to the internal threats of history, maturation, selection, and mortality.

[4]Campbell and Stanley (1993) note that this design is also subject to the internal threats of mortality and the interaction of selection with history, maturation, etc.

[5]You may recall from Topic 32 that a pretest is not essential in a two-group design *if* the subjects are assigned at random to the groups because the random assignment assures that the two groups are initially the same *except for random differences*, which can be assessed with inferential statistics. See the discussion of Design 2 in Topic 32.

new drug to a small group of subjects in order to observe them for side effects, to determine the maximum tolerable dosage, to explore different routes of administration, and so on. The results can be used in planning a subsequent true experiment on the effects of the drug, using a randomized control group.

# EXERCISE ON TOPIC 35

1. Are pre-experimental designs useful for identifying cause-and-effect relationships?

2. Suppose we gave a new program to all students in a school. At the end of the school year, we administered a standardized test to students in the school as well as to students in another school who were serving as a control group. Is the comparison of the average scores for the two groups of students useful for determining the effects of the program?

3. What is the name of the pre-experimental design used in question 2?

4. If a researcher gives a pretest on knowledge of child abuse to a group of social workers, then gives them a series of seminars on child abuse followed by a posttest, what is the name of the pre-experimental design he or she used?

5. Is the design used in question 4 useful for determining cause-and-effect relationships?

## Questions for Discussion

6. Suppose we selected subjects at random from a population and then used the one-group pretest-posttest design. Would the random selection make this design good for exploring cause-and-effect relationships?

7. Have you ever used a pre-experimental design in any of your professional or everyday activities (for example, try doing something in a new way and observing for its effects)? If so, briefly describe it. Discuss whether you inferred that what you did affected the outcome.

## For Students Who Are Planning Research

8. If you will be conducting an experiment, will you be using a pre-experimental design? If yes, explain why you will be using such a design given that they have very serious weaknesses.

# Topic 36  Quasi-Experimental Designs

While true experimental designs are excellent and pre-experimental designs are poor for exploring causal relationships, **quasi-experimental** designs are of intermediate value. In this topic, we will examine only two widely used quasi-experimental designs discussed by Campbell and Stanley.[1]

We saw Design 7 in Topic 33, when we were considering threats to internal validity. It is a widely used quasi-experimental design. It features two intact groups (not assigned at random as indicated by the dashed line) and is known as the **nonequivalent control group design**.

**Design 7:**

$$O \quad X \quad O$$
$$\overline{\cdots\cdots\cdots}$$
$$O \qquad O$$

You may recall that Design 7 is subject to *mortality, selection,* and *interaction of selection* with other threats such as *history*. Thus, it is far from ideal, but superior to the pre-experimental designs, which are not interpretable in terms of causal effects. When random assignment to groups is not possible, Design 7 may be the best we can do.

Even though we did not assign subjects at random to the two groups in Design 7, we might use some form of matching to increase the accuracy of the results. For example, in studying the effects of organizational change in hospitals on patient satisfaction with their experiences in hospitals, we might use the patients in one hospital as the experimental and those in the other as the control group. To form matched groups, we might select a sample from one hospital and determine their status on these demographics: medical condition, age, gender, and socioeconomic status. Then we could handpick subjects in the other hospital who are similar in terms of these demographics. While this might be better than just using unmatched samples from both hospitals, the danger here is that we may not have matched on all variables relevant to the treatment. For instance, in this example, we have not taken into account

whether the patients have insurance or not. Those with and those without insurance may be fundamentally different in their views of patient satisfaction. Obviously, assigning subjects at random to the two conditions (using a true experimental design) would be vastly superior since the random assignment would assure us that the two groups were initially the same on *all variables* except for random differences, whose effects can be assessed with inferential statistics.

Design 8, which is known as the **equivalent time-samples design**, has only one group (or, possibly, only one subject). Treatment conditions are alternated (preferably on a random basis) as indicated in the diagram by alternating $X_1$ (an experimental treatment) with $X_0$ (a control condition or comparison treatment).

**Design 8:**

$$X_0 O \quad X_1 O \quad X_0 O \quad X_1 O$$

The subjects in Design 8 are, in effect, serving as both the control subjects (when they are receiving $X_0$) and the experimental subjects (when they are receiving $X_1$). This is a major advantage because we know that the experimental subjects and control subjects (who are actually the same people) are identical in their genetic characteristics, income level, attitudes, beliefs — in fact, in all ways — at the beginning of the experiment. A major disadvantage of this design is the strong possibility of *multiple-treatment interference*. In this case, the second time the subjects receive $X_1$, they have already been exposed to and possibly changed by the earlier treatments.

Notice that giving the treatments repeatedly strengthens internal validity since it is unlikely that these threats are operating only at the times when $X_1$ is given but not when $X_0$ is given. For example, it is unlikely that subjects mature only at $X_1$ and not at $X_0$. Similarly, it is unlikely that *history* confounds the interpretation by causing changes only when $X_1$ is given.

In psychology, a single-group design in which treatments are alternated is often called an

---

[1]For a discussion of others, see Campbell, D. T. & Stanley, J. C. (1963). *Experimental and quasi-experimental designs for research.* Chicago: Rand McNally.

ABAB design, where A and B indicate alternating treatments. Typically, when this is used, there are multiple initial observations before any treatment is given. These initial observations are called the **baseline**, which determines the typical variation in the behavior of subjects over time before any intervention. For example, perhaps we plan to give rewards for in-seat behavior in a classroom to a hyperactive child. We could measure the amount of out-of-seat behavior on a daily basis for a number of days to determine the natural amount of variation from day to day without treatment. Then, when we introduce the rewards, any changes we see after treatment can be evaluated in terms of the natural variation before treatment—in other words, is the decrease in out-of-seat behavior greater after treatment than the natural day-to-day decreases (and increases) observed during the baseline? Since the ABAB design is essentially the same as Design 8 (with the addition of multiple observations before manipulation with a treatment), it has the same strengths and weaknesses as Design 8.

# Exercise on Topic 36

1. What is the name of the design diagrammed immediately below?

      O  X  O
     ----------------
      O     O

2. In the design shown in question 1, what indicates that the subjects were not assigned at random to the groups?

3. If we use matching to form the two groups in the design in question 1, would the resulting design be superior to a true experimental design?

4. What is a major advantage of the equivalent time-samples design?

5. What is a major disadvantage of the equivalent time-samples design?

6. In psychology, what is an ABAB design?

## Question for Discussion

7. Suppose you observed two classes for baseline data on calling-out behavior (that is, calling out in class when it is inappropriate). In Class A you observe much variation in the amount of calling out from day to day. In Class B, there is little variation—there is about the same amount from one day to the next. In which class would it be desirable to have a longer baseline? Why?

## For Students Who Are Planning Research

8. If you will be conducting an experiment, will you be using a quasi-experimental design? If yes, which one? Why are you using a quasi-experimental design instead of a true experimental one? (See Topic 32.)

# Part F

## Understanding Statistics

In this part, we'll begin by examining the differences between the two major branches of statistics — *descriptive statistics*, which help us summarize and describe data that we've collected, and *inferential statistics*, which help us make inferences from samples to the populations from which they were drawn. Then we will consider basic statistical techniques used in analyzing the results of research.

Because this part is designed to prepare you to comprehend statistics reported in research reports, the emphasis is on understanding their meanings—not on computations. Thus, we will take a conceptual look at statistics and consider computations only when they are needed to help you understand concepts.

**Important Note**

The topics in this part are highly interrelated; in many topics, I have assumed that you have mastered material in the earlier topics. Thus, you are strongly advised to read the topics in the order presented.

# NOTES

# TOPIC 37  DESCRIPTIVE AND INFERENTIAL STATISTICS

**Descriptive statistics** help us summarize data so they can be easily comprehended. For example, suppose we administered a test to all 362 freshmen enrolled in a university. An unordered list of the scores would be difficult to process mentally. However, if we prepare a frequency distribution such as that in Table 1, we can easily see how the scores are distributed. For example, the table clearly indicates that a majority had scores of 14 through 16, with a scattering above and below these levels.

Table 1  *Frequency distribution with percentages*

| Score ($X$) | Frequency ($f$) | Percentage |
|:---:|:---:|:---:|
| 20 | 5 | 1.4 |
| 19 | 9 | 2.5 |
| 18 | 24 | 6.6 |
| 17 | 35 | 9.7 |
| 16 | 61 | 16.9 |
| 15 | 99 | 27.3 |
| 14 | 68 | 18.8 |
| 13 | 29 | 8.0 |
| 12 | 21 | 5.8 |
| 11 | 11 | 3.0 |
| Total | 362 | 100.0% |

The frequencies in Table 1 are descriptive statistics; they describe how many students earned each score. The percentages are also descriptive; they describe how many students *per one hundred* had each score. These and other descriptive statistics such as averages are described in this part of the book.

Now let's suppose that for the sake of efficiency, instead of testing all 362 freshmen, we sampled at random (by drawing names out of a hat) only 100 to be tested. Would we obtain exactly the same results as we would if we tested all freshmen? In all likelihood, no. As you probably recall from Topics 17 through 19, random sampling produces random errors called *sampling errors*. **Inferential statistics** help us draw inferences about the effects of sampling errors on our results. They are defined as statistical techniques that help us generalize from samples to the populations from which the samples were drawn.

One type of inferential statistic you may already be familiar with is a *margin of error*. When reporting the results of public opinion polls in the media, reporters frequently cite margins of error to help us interpret results in light of sampling error. For example, a recent poll indicated that approval of the president was at 52% with a margin of error of ±2 (i.e., plus/minus 2) percentage points. This means we can be highly confident that the level of approval in the population is between 50% and 54% (that is, within two points of the 52% observed in the sample).

An important family of inferential statistics consists of *significance tests*, which help us decide whether differences that we observe (such as differences in the reading achievement of samples of boys and girls) are reliable. The next topic will help you understand the general purpose of significance testing, and in later sections, we will consider three popular tests of significance.

Because inferential statistics help us evaluate results in light of sampling errors, it follows that if we do *not* sample, we do *not* need inferential statistics. For example, if we conduct a *census* (a study in which all members of a population are included), the descriptive values that we obtain such as percentages are values that are free of sampling errors.

We distinguish between values obtained from a sample and values obtained from a census by using the terms **parameters** for values from a census and **statistics** for values from studies in which samples were examined. Thus, percentages, averages, and frequencies are classified as parameters when they result from a census, but they are classified as statistics when they are based on a sample. Remember the first letters:

**S**amples yield **S**tatistics, and
**P**opulations yield **P**arameters.

# Exercise on Topic 37

1. Which branch of statistics helps us summarize data so they can be easily comprehended?

2. According to Table 1 in this topic, how many subjects had a score of 19?

3. What is the name of the statistic that describes how many subjects per 100 have a certain characteristic?

4. Which branch of statistics helps us draw inferences about the effects of sampling errors on our results?

5. If we test a random sample instead of all members of a population, is it likely that the sample results will be the same as the results we would have obtained by testing the population?

6. Is a margin of error a descriptive or an inferential statistic?

7. Do we perform significance tests with inferential or descriptive statistics?

8. By studying populations, do we obtain statistics or parameters?

9. By studying samples, do we obtain statistics or parameters?

## Question for Discussion

10. Keep your eye out for a report of a poll in which a margin of error is reported. Copy the exact words and bring it to class for discussion.

## For Students Who Are Planning Research

11. Will you be reporting descriptive statistics? (Note that statistics often are not reported in qualitative research. See Topics 9 and 10.)

12. Will you be reporting inferential statistics? (Note that they are needed only if you have sampled.)

Suppose we drew random samples of engineers and psychologists, administered a self-report measure of sociability, and computed the mean (the most commonly used average) for each group. Furthermore, suppose the mean for engineers is 65.00 and the mean for psychologists is 70.00. Where did the five-point difference come from? There are three possible explanations:

1. Perhaps the population of psychologists is truly more sociable than the population of engineers, and our samples correctly identified the difference. (In fact, our *research hypothesis* may have been that psychologists are more sociable than engineers—which now appears to be supported by the data.)

2. Perhaps there was a bias in procedures. By using random sampling, we have ruled out sampling bias, but other procedures such as measurement may be biased. For example, maybe the psychologists were contacted during December, when many social events take place and the engineers were contacted during a gloomy February. The only way to rule out bias as an explanation is to take *physical steps* to prevent it. In this case, we would want to make sure that the sociability of both groups was measured in the same way at the same time.

3. Perhaps the populations of psychologists and engineers are the same but the samples are unrepresentative of their populations because of random sampling errors. For instance, the random draw may have given us a sample of psychologists who are more sociable, on the average, than their population.

The third explanation has a name—it is the **null hypothesis**. The general form in which it is stated varies from researcher to researcher. Here are three versions, all of which are consistent with each other:

**Version A of the null hypothesis:**
*The observed difference was created by sampling error.* (Note that the term *sampling error*

refers only to *random errors*—not errors created by a bias.)

**Version B of the null hypothesis:**
*There is no true difference between the two groups.* (The term *true difference* refers to the difference we would find in a census of the populations, that is, the difference we would find if there were no sampling errors.)

**Version C of the null hypothesis:**
*The true difference between the two groups is zero.*

*Significance tests* determine the probability that the null hypothesis is true. (We will be considering the use of specific significance tests in Topics 41–42 and 48–50.) Suppose for our example we use a significance test and find that the probability that the null hypothesis is true is less than 5 in 100; this would be stated as $p < .05$, where $p$ obviously stands for *probability*. Of course, if the chances that something is true is less than 5 in 100, it's a good bet that it's *not* true. If it's probably not true, we *reject the null hypothesis*, leaving us with only the first two explanations that we started with as viable explanations for the difference.

There is no rule of nature that dictates at what probability level the null hypothesis should be rejected. However, conventional wisdom suggests that .05 or less (such as .01 or .001) is reasonable. Of course, researchers should state in their reports the probability level they used to determine whether to reject the null hypothesis.

Note that when we fail to reject the null hypothesis because the probability is greater than .05, we do just that: We "fail to reject" the null hypothesis and it stays on our list of possible explanations; we *never* "accept" the null hypothesis as the only explanation—remember, there are three possible explanations and failing to reject one of them does not mean that you are accepting it as the only explanation.

An alternative way to say that we have rejected the null hypothesis is to state that the difference is *statistically significant*. Thus, if we state that a difference is statistically significant at the .05 level (meaning .05 or less), it is equivalent to stating that the null hypothesis has been rejected at that level.

When you read research reported in academic journals, you will find that the null hypothesis is seldom stated by researchers, who assume that you know that the sole purpose of a significance test is to test a null hypothesis. Instead, researchers tell you which differences were tested for significance, which significance test they used, and which differences were found to be statistically significant. It is more common to find null hypotheses stated in theses and dissertations since committee members may wish to make sure that the students they are supervising understand the reason they have conducted a significance test.

As we consider specific significance tests in the next three parts of this book, we'll examine the null hypothesis in more detail.

# EXERCISE ON TOPIC 38

1. How many explanations were there for the difference in sociability between psychologists and engineers in the example in this topic?

2. What does the null hypothesis say about sampling error?

3. Does the term *sampling error* refer to *random errors* or to *bias*?

4. The null hypothesis says that the true difference equals what value?

5. What is used to determine the probabilities that null hypotheses are true?

6. For what does $p < .05$ stand?

7. Do we reject the null hypothesis when the probability of its truth is high or when it is low?

8. What do we do if the probability is greater than .05?

9. What is an alternative way of saying that we have rejected the null hypothesis?

10. Are you more likely to find a null hypothesis stated in a journal article or in a thesis?

## Question for Discussion

11. We all use probabilities in everyday activities to make decisions. For example, before we cross a busy street, we estimate the odds that we will get across the street safely. Briefly describe one other specific use of probability in everyday decision making.

## For Students Who Are Planning Research

12. Will you need to test the null hypothesis in your research? Explain.

# TOPIC 39  SCALES OF MEASUREMENT

There are four scales (or levels) at which we measure. The lowest level is the **nominal** scale. This may be thought of as the "naming" level. For example, when we ask subjects to name their marital status, they will respond with *words*—not numbers—that describe their status such as "married," "single," "divorced," etc. Notice that nominal data do not put subjects in any particular order. There is no logical basis for saying that one category such as "single" is higher or lower than any other.

The next level is **ordinal**. At this level, we put subjects in order from high to low. For instance, an employer might rank order applicants for a job on their professional appearance. Traditionally, we give a rank of 1 to the subject who is highest, 2 to the next highest, and so on. It is important to note that ranks do not tell us by how much subjects differ. If we are told that Janet has a rank of 1 and Frank has a rank of 2, we do not know if Janet's appearance is greatly superior to Frank's or only slightly superior. To measure the *amount* of difference among subjects, we use the next levels of measurement.

Measurements at the **interval** and **ratio** levels have equal distances among the scores they yield. For example, when we say that Jill weighs 120 pounds and Sally weighs 130 pounds, we know by *how much* the two subjects differ. Also, note that a 10-pound difference represents the same amount regardless of where we are on the scale. For instance, the difference between 120 and 130 pounds is the same as the difference between 220 and 230 pounds.

The ratio scale is at a higher level than the interval scale because the ratio has an absolute zero point that we know how to measure. Thus, *weight* is an example of the ratio scale because it has an absolute zero that we can measure.

The interval scale, while having equal intervals like the ratio scale, does not have an absolute zero. The most common examples of interval scales are scores obtained using objective tests such as multiple-choice tests of achievement. It is widely assumed that each multiple-choice test item measures a single point's worth of the trait

being measured and that all points are equal to all other points—making it an interval scale (just as all pounds are equal to all other pounds of weight). However, such tests do not measure at the ratio level because the zero on such tests is arbitrary—not absolute. To see this, consider someone who gets a zero on a multiple-choice final examination. Does the zero mean that the student has absolutely no knowledge of or skills in the subject area? Probably not. He or she probably has some knowledge of simple facts, definitions, and concepts, but the test was not designed to measure at the skill level at which the student is operating. Thus, a score of zero indicates only that the student knows nothing *on that test*—not that the student has zero knowledge of the content domain.

Here's a summary of the levels:

| Lowest Level | Scale | Characteristic |
|---|---|---|
| | **Nominal** | *naming* |
| | **Ordinal** | *ordering* |
| ⇓ | **Interval** | *equal interval without absolute zero* |
| | **Ratio** | *equal interval with absolute zero* |
| Highest Level | | |

For those of you who like to use mnemonics when memorizing material, try learning this environmentally friendly phrase:

## No Oil In Rivers

The first letters—**NOIR**—are the first letters of the scales in order from lowest to highest.

At which level should we measure? First, some variables are inherently nominal in nature. For example, when we need to know subjects' gender or state of residence, nominal data is the natural choice. Second, many novice researchers overuse the ordinal scale. For instance, if we want to measure reading ability, it usually would be much better to use a carefully constructed standardized test (which measures at the interval level) than having teachers rank order students in terms of their reading ability. Remember, measuring at the interval level gives you more information because it tells you by *how much* students differ. Also, as you will learn when we explore statistics, you can do more interesting and powerful types of analyses when you measure at the interval rather than the ordinal level. Thus, when planning instruments for a research project, if you are thinking in terms of having subjects ranked (for ordinal measurement), you would be well advised to consider whether there is an alternative at the interval level.

The choice between interval and ratio depends solely on whether it is possible to measure with an absolute zero. When it is possible, we usually do so. For the purposes of statistical analysis, interval and ratio data are treated in the same way.

The level at which we measure has important implications for data analysis, so you will find references to scales of measurement throughout our discussion of statistics.

# EXERCISE ON TOPIC 39

1. If we ask subjects to name the country in which they were born, we are using what scale of measurement?

2. Which two scales of measurement have equal distances among the scores they yield?

3. If we have a teacher rank students according to their oral language skills, we are using which scale of measurement?

4. Which scale of measurement has an absolute zero that is measured?

5. Which scale of measurement is at the lowest level?

6. Objective, multiple-choice achievement tests are usually assumed to measure at what level?

7. If we measure in such a way that we find out which subject is most honest, which is the next most honest, and so on, we are measuring at what scale of measurement?

8. The number of minutes of overtime work that employees perform is an example of what scale of measurement?

9. Weight measured in pounds is an example of which scale of measurement?

## Question for Discussion

10. Name a trait that inherently lends itself to nominal measurement. Explain your answer.

## For Students Who Are Planning Research

11. List the measures you will be using, and name the scale of measurement for each one.

# Topic 40   Descriptions of Nominal Data

We obtain *nominal data* when we classify subjects according to names (words) instead of quantities. For example, suppose we asked a population of 540 teachers which candidate they each prefer for a school board vacancy and found that 258 preferred Smith and 282 preferred Jones. The 258 and 282 are **frequencies**, whose symbol is *f*; we can also refer to them as **numbers of cases**, whose symbol is *N*.

We can convert the numbers of cases into **percentages** by dividing the number who prefer each candidate by the number in the population and multiplying by 100. Thus, for Smith, the calculations are:

$$258 \div 540 = .478 \times 100 = 47.8\%$$

When reporting percentages, it's a good idea to also report the underlying numbers of cases, which is done in Table 1.

Table 1 *Teachers' preferences*

| Candidate | |
| --- | --- |
| Jones | 52.2% (N = 282) |
| Smith | 47.8% (N = 258) |
| Total | 100.0% |

Table 1 is an example of *univariate analysis*. We are analyzing how people *vary* (hence, we use the root *variate*) on only *one* variable (hence, we use the prefix *uni-*).

We can examine a *relationship* between two nominal variables by conducting a bivariate analysis. Perhaps we want to know whether there is a relationship between teachers' gender and their preferences for candidates. Table 2 shows the results of a bivariate analysis of these variables.

The data in Table 2 clearly indicate that there is a relationship between gender and preference for either Jones or Smith. A larger percentage of males than females prefers Jones, but a larger percentage of females than males prefers Smith. Another way to put this is that teachers' gender is

Table 2 *Teachers' preferences by gender*

| | Jones | Smith | Total |
| --- | --- | --- | --- |
| Male | 66.4% (N = 85) | 33.6% (N = 43) | 100.0% (N = 128) |
| Female | 47.8% (N = 197) | 52.2% (N = 215) | 100.0% (N = 412) |

predictive of their preferences. For instance, by knowing that a teacher is male, we would predict that he is more likely to vote for Jones than Smith.

Notice that in this population of teachers, there are many more female teachers than male teachers. When this is the case, we can be misled by examining only the numbers of cases (for example, 85 males for Jones versus 197 females for Jones). Notice that, in fact, a *majority* of the smaller population of males is in favor of Jones but only a *minority* of the larger population of females is in favor of him. With percentages, legitimate comparisons of groups of unequal size are possible. This is because percentages convert numbers of cases to a common scale with a base of 100. (The percentage of 66.4% of males for Jones indicates that *for every 100 males*, 66.4 of them are in favor of Jones while the percentage of 47.8% of females for Jones indicates that *for every 100 females*, only 47.8 of them are in favor of Jones.)

In academic writing, some researchers report the **proportions** instead of the *percentages*. For example, a percentage of 47.8% in favor of Smith in Table 1 corresponds to a proportion of .478 or .48. (Proportions are calculated in the same way percentages are except that we do not multiply by 100.) Since a proportion has a base of 1, a proportion of .48 means that for every *one* subject, 48 hundredths of each subject favors Smith. Clearly, proportions are harder to comprehend than percentages. When you encounter proportions in literature, it's a good idea to convert them mentally to percentages. That is, think of .48 as 48% (the percentage you get by multiplying by 100).

In the next section, we will consider how to analyze nominal data in studies in which we have sampled at random and need to take account of random sampling errors.

# Exercise on Topic 40

1. If 400 people in a population of 1,000 are Democrats, what percentage are Democrats?

2. When reporting a percentage, is it a good idea to also report the underlying number of cases?

3. Do we use univariate or bivariate analyses to examine relationships among nominal variables?

4. Percentages convert numbers of cases to a common scale with what base?

5. What is the base for a proportion?

6. Are percentages or proportions easier for most people to comprehend?

## Question for Discussion

7. Be on the lookout for a report in the popular press in which percentages are reported. Bring a copy to class. Be prepared to discuss whether the frequencies are also reported and whether it is a univariate or bivariate analysis.

## For Students Who Are Planning Research

8. Will you be measuring anything at the nominal level? Explain.

9. Will you be reporting percentages? Will you do a univariate analysis? A bivariate analysis? Explain.

# TOPIC 41 INTRODUCTION TO THE CHI SQUARE TEST

Suppose we drew at random a sample of 200 members of a professional association of sociologists and asked them whether they were in favor of a proposed change to their bylaws. The results are shown in Table 1. But do these *observed results*[1] reflect the *true results* that we would have obtained if we had questioned the entire population? Remember that the null hypothesis (see Topic 38) says that the observed difference was created by random sampling errors; that is, in the population, the true difference is zero. Put another way, the observed difference ($n = 120$ vs. $n = 80$) is an *illusion* created by chance errors.

Table 1 *Members' approval of a change in bylaws*

| Response | |
|---|---|
| Yes | 60.0% |
| | ($n = 120$) |
| No | 40.0% |
| | ($n = 80$) |
| Total | 100.0% |

The usual test of the null hypothesis when we are considering frequencies (that is, number of cases or $n$) is **chi square**, whose symbol is:

$$\chi^2$$

It turns out that after doing some computations, which are beyond the scope of this book, for the data in Table 1, the results are:

$$\chi^2 = 4.00, df = 1, p < .05$$

What does this mean for a consumer of research who sees this in a report? The values of chi square and degrees of freedom ($df$) were calculated solely to obtain the probability that the null hypothesis is correct. That is, chi square and degrees of freedom are *not* descriptive statistics that you should attempt to interpret. Rather, think of them as substeps in the mathematical procedure for obtaining the value of $p$. Thus, the consumer of research should concentrate on the fact that $p$ is *less than*

.05. As you probably recall from Topic 38, when the probability ($p$) that the null hypothesis is correct is .05 or less, we reject the null hypothesis. (Remember, when the probability that something is true is less than 5 in 100—a low probability—conventional wisdom suggests that we should reject it as being true.) Thus, the difference we observe in Table 1 was probably not created by random sampling errors; therefore, we can say that the difference is *statistically significant* at the .05 level.

So far, we have concluded that the difference we observed in the sample was *probably not* created by sampling errors. So where did the difference come from? Two possibilities remain:

1. Perhaps there was a bias in procedures such as the person asking the question in the survey leading the respondents by talking enthusiastically about the proposed change in the bylaws. If we are convinced that adequate measures were taken to prevent procedural bias, we are left with only the next possibility as a viable explanation.

2. Perhaps the *population* of sociologists is, in fact, in favor of the proposed change, and this fact is correctly identified by studying the random sample.

Now let's consider some results from a survey in which the null hypothesis was *not* rejected. Table 2 shows the numbers and percentages of subjects in a random sample from a population of teachers who prefer each of three methods for teaching reading. In the table, there are three differences (30 for A versus 27 for B, 30 for A versus 22 for C, and 27 for B versus 22 for C). The null hypothesis says that this *set of differences* was created by random sampling errors; in other

Table 2 *Teachers' preferences for methods*

| Method A | Method B | Method C |
|---|---|---|
| $n = 30$ (37.97%) | $n = 27$ (34.18%) | $n = 22$ (27.85%) |

---

[1]We are using the term *true results* here to stand for the results of a census of the entire population. The results of a census are *true* in the sense that they are free of *sampling errors*. Of course, there may also be measurement errors, which we are not considering here.

words, it says that there is no true difference in the population; we have observed a difference only because of sampling errors. The results of the chi square test for the data in Table 2 are:

$$\chi^2 = 1.214, df = 2, p > .05$$

Using the decision rule that $p$ must be equal to or less than .05 to reject the null hypothesis, we *fail to reject the null hypothesis*, which is called a statistically *in*significant result. In other words, the null hypothesis must remain on our list as a viable explanation for the set of differences we observed by studying a sample.

In this topic, we have considered the use of chi square in a *univariate analysis* in which we classify each subject in only one way (such as which candidate each prefers). In the next topic, we'll consider its use in *bivariate analysis* in which we classify each subject in two ways (such as which candidate each prefers *and* the gender of each) in order to examine a relationship between the two.

# EXERCISE ON TOPIC 41

1. When we study a sample, are the results called the *true results* or the *observed results*?

2. According to the null hypothesis, what created the difference in Table 1 in this topic?

3. What is the name of the test of the null hypothesis used when we are analyzing frequencies?

4. As a consumer of research, should you try to interpret the value of *df*?

5. What is the symbol for *probability*?

6. If you read that a chi square test of a difference yielded a *p* of less than 5 in 100, what should you conclude about the null hypothesis on the basis of conventional wisdom?

7. Does $p < .05$ or $p > .05$ usually lead a researcher to declare a difference to be statistically significant?

8. If we fail to reject a null hypothesis, is the difference in question statistically significant?

9. If we have a statistically insignificant result, does the null hypothesis remain on our list of viable hypotheses?

## Question for Discussion

10. Briefly describe a hypothetical study in which it would be appropriate to conduct a chi square test for univariate data.

## For Students Who Are Planning Research

11. Will you be conducting a chi square test? Explain.

# Topic 42  A Closer Look at the Chi Square Test

In this topic, we will examine the use of the chi square test in a *bivariate analysis* — that is, when each subject is classified in terms of two variables in order to examine the relationship between them. Let's look at an example. Suppose we conducted an experiment in which three methods of job training were tried with welfare recipients. Random samples of recipients were drawn for each method, and the number who obtained jobs by the end of the training sessions was determined. The resulting data are shown in Table 1.

Table 1  *Training methods and job placement*

| Job? | Method A | Method B | Method C |
|---|---|---|---|
| Yes | $n = 20$ (66.7%) | $n = 15$ (51.7%) | $n = 9$ (31.0%) |
| No | $n = 10$ (33.3%) | $n = 14$ (48.3%) | $n = 20$ (69.0%) |

Clearly, the data suggest that there is a relationship between which method of job training was used and the outcome (whether or not subjects got jobs). Based on the random samples, it appears that Method A is superior to Methods B and C and that Method B is superior to Method C. A stumbling block in our interpretation of these results is the *null hypothesis*, which says that there is no true difference (that is, if all members of the population had been studied, we would have found no differences among the three methods). For instance, quite by the luck of the random draw, recipients who were more employable to begin with (before treatment) were assigned to Method A, while the less employable, by chance, were assigned to the other two methods. We can test the null hypothesis by using chi square.

For the data shown in Table 1, this result would be shown in a report on the experiment:

$$\chi^2 = 7.54, df = 2, p < .05$$

As you know from the previous topics, we reject the null hypothesis when the odds that it is true are equal to or less than .05. Thus, for this data, we reject the null hypothesis and declare the result to be significant at the .05 level. We have concluded that the observed differences that suggest a relationship between method of training and job placement are too great to be attributed to random errors.

Now let's consider what we mean by the .05 level in more detail than we have up to this point. When we reject the null hypothesis at exactly the .05 level (that is, $p = .05$), there are 5 chances in 100 that the null hypothesis is correct; thus, we are taking 5 chances in 100 of being *wrong* by rejecting null hypotheses at this level. In other words, we can never be certain that we have made the correct decision when rejecting the null hypothesis. It is always possible that the null hypothesis is true (in this case, there are 5 in 100 chances that it is true), and that we are making a mistake by rejecting it. This possibility is called a *Type I Error*. When we use the .05 level, the odds of making a Type I Error are 5 in 100; when we use the .01 level, the odds of making this type of error are 1 in 100; and when we use the .001 level, the odds of making it are 1 in 1,000.

When we fail to reject the null hypothesis, as we did in Topic 41 for the data in Table 2, we also are taking a chance that we are wrong. That is, perhaps the null hypothesis should have been rejected, but the significance test failed to lead us to the correct decision. This mistake is called a *Type II Error*. In review, these are the two types of errors:

**Type I Error:** Rejecting the null hypothesis when it is, in fact, a correct hypothesis.

**Type II Error:** Failing to reject the null hypothesis when it is, in fact, an incorrect hypothesis.

At first, this discussion of errors may make significance tests such as chi square seem weak—after all, we can be wrong no matter what decision we make. But let's look at the big picture. Once we decide to sample at random (the desirable way to sample because it's free from bias), we are open to the possibility that random errors have influenced our results. From this point on, we can never be *certain*. Instead, we must use *probabilities* to make decisions. We use them in such a way that we *minimize* the probability that we are wrong. To do this, we usually emphasize minimizing the probability of a Type I Error by using a low probability such as .05 or less. By using a low probability, we will infrequently be wrong in rejecting the null hypothesis.

# EXERCISE ON TOPIC 42

1. What is the name of the type of analysis when each subject is classified in terms of two variables in order to examine the relationship between them?

2. What decision have we made about the null hypothesis if a chi square test leads us to the conclusion that the observed differences that suggest a relationship between two variables are too great to be attributed to random errors?

3. If $p = .05$ for a chi square test, chances are how many in 100 that the null hypothesis is true?

4. When we use the .01 level, what are the odds of making a Type I Error?

5. What is the name for the error we make when we fail to reject the null hypothesis when it is, in fact, an incorrect hypothesis?

6. What is the name for the error we make when we reject the null hypothesis when it is, in fact, a correct hypothesis?

7. Why is random sampling desirable even though it creates errors?

## Questions for Discussion

8. Are both of the variables in Table 1 in this topic nominal? Explain.

9. Briefly describe a hypothetical study in which it would be appropriate to conduct a chi square test on bivariate data.

## For Students Who Are Planning Research

10. Will you be using a chi square test in a bivariate analysis? Explain.

# TOPIC 43  SHAPES OF DISTRIBUTIONS

One way to describe quantitative data is to prepare a *frequency distribution* such as that shown in Topic 37 (see page 91). It is easier to see the shape of the distribution if we prepare a figure called a **frequency polygon**. This figure is a frequency polygon for the data in Topic 37:

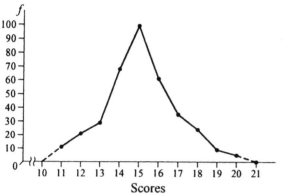

Figure 1  *Frequency polygon for data on page 91*

A frequency polygon is easy to read. For example, a score of 20 has a frequency (*f*) of 5, which is why the curve is low at a score of 20. A score of 15 has a frequency of 99, which is why the curve is high at 15.

Notice that the curve in Figure 1 is fairly symmetrical with a high point in the middle and dropping off on the right and left. When very large samples are used, the curve often takes on an even smoother shape, such as the one shown in Figure 2.

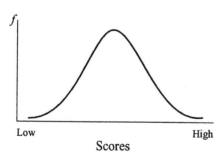

Figure 2  *The normal curve*

The smooth, bell-shaped curve in Figure 2 has a special name; it is the **normal curve**. As the name "normal" suggests, it is the common shape that is regularly observed. Many things in nature are normally distributed—the weights of grains of sand on a beach, the heights of women (or men), the annual amounts of rainfall in most areas, and so on. The list is almost limitless. Many social and behavioral scientists also believe that mental traits of humans probably are also normally distributed.[1]

Some distributions are **skewed**—that is, they have a tail to the left or right. Figure 3 shows a distribution that is *skewed to the right* (that is , the tail is to the right); it is said to have a **positive skew**. An example of a distribution with a positive skew is income. Most people earn relatively small amounts, so the curve is high on the left. Small numbers of rich and very rich people create a tail to the right.

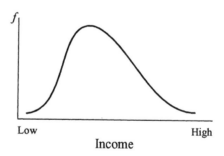

Figure 3  *A distribution with a positive skew*

Figure 4 is *skewed to the left*; it has a **negative skew**. We would get a negative skew, for example, if we administered a test of basic math skills to a large sample of college seniors. Most would do very well and get almost perfect scores, but a small scattering will get lower scores for a variety of reasons such as misunderstanding the directions for marking their answers, not feeling well the day the test was administered, and so on.

---

[1]Because measures of mental traits are far from perfect, it is difficult to show conclusively that mental traits are normally distributed. However, many norm-referenced tests do yield normal distributions when large representative national samples are tested.

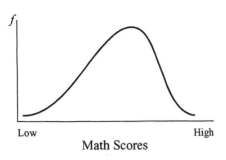

Low                High
Math Scores

Figure 4   *A distribution with a negative skew*

While there are other shapes, the three shown here are the ones you are most likely to encounter. Whether a distribution is basically normal or skewed affects how quantitative data at the interval and ratio levels are analyzed, which we will consider in the next topic.

# EXERCISE ON TOPIC 43

1. According to Figure 1, about how many subjects had a score of 14?

2. In Figure 1, are the frequencies on the vertical or horizontal axis?

3. Which of the curves discussed in this topic is symmetrical?

4. If a distribution has some extreme scores on the right (but not on the left) it is said to have what type of skew?

5. If a distribution is skewed to the left, does it have a positive or negative skew?

6. In most populations, income has what type of skew?

7. Does a distribution with a tail to the right have a positive or negative skew?

## Question for Discussion

8. Name a population and a variable that might be measured. Speculate on whether the distribution would be normal or skewed.

## For Students Who Are Planning Research

9. Do you anticipate that any of your distributions will be highly skewed? Explain.

# TOPIC 44  THE MEAN, MEDIAN, AND MODE

The most frequently used average is the **mean**, which is the *balance point* in a distribution. Its computation is simple—just sum (add up) the scores and divide by the number of scores. The most common symbol for the mean in academic journals is $M$ (for the mean of a population) or $m$ (for the mean of a sample). The symbol preferred by statisticians is

$\overline{X}$ which is pronounced "X-bar."

Because the mean is very frequently used as the average, let's consider its *formal definition*, which is *the value around which the deviations sum to zero*. You can see what this means by considering the scores in Table 1. When we subtract the mean of the scores (which is 4.0) from each of the other scores, we get the deviations (whose symbol is $x$). If we sum the deviations, we get zero, as shown in Table 1.

Table 1  *Scores and deviation scores*

| $X$ | minus | $M$ | equals | $x$ |
|---|---|---|---|---|
| 1 | – | 4.0 | = | -3.0 |
| 1 | – | 4.0 | = | -3.0 |
| 1 | – | 4.0 | = | -3.0 |
| 2 | – | 4.0 | = | -2.0 |
| 2 | – | 4.0 | = | -2.0 |
| 4 | – | 4.0 | = | 0.0 |
| 6 | – | 4.0 | = | 2.0 |
| 7 | – | 4.0 | = | 3.0 |
| 8 | – | 4.0 | = | 4.0 |
| 8 | – | 4.0 | = | 4.0 |
| **Sum of the deviations ($x$) =** | | | | **0.0** |

Note that if you take *any set of scores*, compute their mean, and follow the steps in Table 1, the sum of the deviations will always equal zero.[1]

Considering the formal definition, you can see why we also informally define the mean as the *balance point* in a distribution. The positive and negative deviations *balance* each other out.

A major drawback of the mean is that it is drawn in the direction of extreme scores. Consider the following two sets of scores and their means.

**Scores for Group A:** 1, 1, 1, 2, 3, 6, 7, 8, 8
$M = 4.11$

**Scores for Group B:** 1, 2, 2, 3, 4, 7, 9, 25, 32
$M = 9.44$

Notice that in both sets there are nine scores and the two distributions are very similar except for the scores of 25 and 32 in Group B, which are much higher than the others and, thus, create a skewed distribution. (To review skewed distributions, see Topic 43.) Notice that the two very high scores have greatly pulled up the mean for Group B; in fact, the mean for Group B is more than twice as high as the mean for Group A because of the two high scores.

When a distribution is highly skewed, we use a different average, the **median**, which is defined as the *middle score*. To get an *approximate median*, put the scores in order from low to high as they are for Groups A and B above, and then count to the middle. Since there are nine scores in Group A, the median (middle score) is 3 (five scores up from the bottom). For Group B, the median (middle score) is 4 (five scores up from the bottom), which is more representative of the center of this skewed distribution than the mean, which we noted was 9.44. Thus, one use of the median is to describe the average of skewed distributions. Another use is to describe the average of ordinal data, which we'll explore in Topic 46.

A third average, the **mode**, is simply the *most frequently occurring score*. For Group B, there are more scores of 2 than any other score; thus, 2 is the mode. The mode is sometimes used in informal reporting but is very seldom used in formal reports of research.

Because there is more than one type of average, it is vague to make a statement such as, "The *average* is 4.11." Rather, we should indicate the specific type of average being reported with statements such as, "The *mean* is 4.11."

---

[1] It might be slightly off from zero if you use a rounded mean such as using 20.33 as the mean when its precise value is 20.3333333333.

Note that a synonym for the term **averages** is **measures of central tendency**. Although the latter is seldom used in reports of scientific research, you may encounter it in other research and statistics textbooks.

# EXERCISE ON TOPIC 44

1. Which average is defined as the *most frequently occurring score*?

2. Which average is defined as the *balance point* in a distribution?

3. Which average is defined as the *middle score*?

4. What is the formal definition of the mean?

5. How is the mean calculated?

6. Should the mean be used for highly skewed distributions?

7. Should the median be used for highly skewed distributions?

8. What is a synonym for the term *averages*?

## Question for Discussion

9. Suppose a fellow student gave a report in class and said, "The average was 25.88." For what additional information should you ask? Why?

## For Students Who Are Planning Research

10. Do you anticipate calculating measure(s) of central tendency? If so, which one(s) are you likely to use? Explain your choice(s).

# Topic 45 The Mean and Standard Deviation

Often, a distribution of scores is described with only two statistics: the **mean** to describe its *average*, and the **standard deviation** (whose symbol is *S* or *SD* for a population, and *s* or *sd* for a sample) to describe its *variability*. What do we mean by variability? It refers to the amount by which subjects *vary* or differ from each other. Let's see what this means by considering three groups, all of which have the same mean but different standard deviations.

**Group A:** 0, 5, 10, 15, 20, 25, 30
$M = 15.00, S = 10.00$

**Group B:** 14, 14, 14, 15, 16, 16, 16
$M = 15.00, S = 0.93$

**Group C:** 15, 15, 15, 15, 15, 15, 15
$M = 15.00, S = 0.00$

Although the three groups are the same on the average, as indicated by the mean, they are very different in terms of variability. Notice that the differences among the scores of Group A (a score of 0 vs. a score of 5 vs. a score of 10 vs. a score of 15, etc.) are much greater than the differences among the scores of Group B (a score of 14 vs. a score of 14 vs. a score of 14 vs. a score of 15, etc.). At the extreme, when all the scores are the same, as in Group C, the standard deviation equals zero. Thus, you can see, the smaller the standard deviation, the smaller the variability.[1]

The standard deviation has a special relationship to the normal curve (see Topic 43). *If a distribution is normal, 68% of the subjects in the distribution lies within one standard deviation unit of the mean.*[2] For example, if you read in a report that $M = 70$ and $S = 10$ for a normal distribution, you would know that 68% of the subjects have scores between 60 and 80 (that is, $70 - 10 = 60$ and $70 + 10 = 80$). This is illustrated in Figure 1.

In Figure 2, the mean is also 70, but the standard deviation is only 5. The smaller standard deviation in Figure 2 is reflected by the fact that the curve is narrower than in Figure 1. Yet, in both distributions, 68% of the cases lies within one standard deviation unit of the mean because they are both normal.

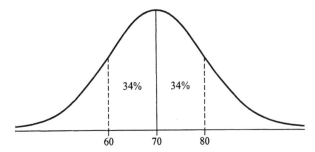

Figure 1 *Normal curve with a standard deviation of 10*

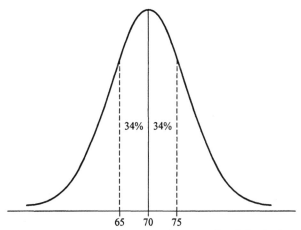

Figure 2 *Normal curve with a standard deviation of 5*

At first this seems like magic—regardless of the value of the standard deviation, 68% of the cases lies within one standard deviation unit in a normal curve. Actually, it is not magic but a property of the normal curve. When you are calculating the standard deviation, you are actually calculating the number of points that one must go out from the mean to capture 68% of the cases. This 68% rule does *not* strictly apply if the distribution is *not* normal. The less normal it is, the less accurate the rule is.

---

[1]For those of you who are mathematically inclined, the computation of the standard deviation is illustrated in Appendix F. Considering how it is computed may give you a better feeling for its meaning.
[2]Note that *within* means on *both sides of the mean*, that is, the standard deviation plus/minus the mean.

# EXERCISE ON TOPIC 45

1. Which average is usually reported when the standard deviation is reported?

2. What is meant by the term *variability*?

3. Is it possible for two groups to have the same mean but different standard deviations?

4. If everyone in a group has the same score, what is the value of the standard deviation for the scores?

5. What percentage of the subjects lies within one standard deviation unit of the mean in a normal distribution?

6. The middle 68% of the subjects in a normal distribution has scores between what two values if the mean equals 100 and the standard deviation equals 15?

7. If the mean of a normal distribution equals 50 and the standard deviation equals 5, what percentage of the subjects has scores between 45 and 50?

8. Does the 68% rule strictly apply if a distribution is *not* normal?

9. If the standard deviation for Group X is 14.55 and the standard deviation for Group Y is 20.99, which group has less variability in their scores?

10. Which group in question 9 has a narrower curve?

## Question for Discussion

11. Examine a journal article in which a mean and standard deviation are reported. Does the author indicate whether the distribution is normal in shape? Does the 68% rule strictly apply? Explain.

## For Students Who Are Planning Research

12. Will you be reporting means and standard deviations? Explain.

# Topic 46  The Median and Interquartile Range

As you know from Topic 44, the **median** is the *middle score* in a distribution. Being in the middle, it always has 50% of the scores above it and 50% of the scores below it. For the scores in Figure 1, the median is 6.5 (halfway between the middle two scores of 6 and 7).

1, 1, 1, 2, 3, 4, 5, 6, 7, 8, 8, 9, 10, 11, 11, 12
⇑
6.5

Figure 1  *Scores for Group A and their median*

The median is used instead of the mean when a distribution is highly skewed (see Topic 43). It is also used to describe the average of a set of *ordinal* data (that is, data that put subjects in *order* from high to low but do not have equal intervals among them; see Topic 39).[1]

When the **median** is reported as the average, it is customary to report the **range** or **interquartile range** as a measure of variability. You should recall from Topic 45 that *variability* refers to the amount by which subjects *vary* or differ from each other.

The *range* is simply the highest score minus the lowest score. For the scores shown above, it is 12 − 1 = 11 (or we can say that the scores *range from* 1 to 12). For reasons that are beyond the scope of this discussion, measurement theory tells us that the more extreme the score, the more unreliable it is. Since the range is based on the two most extreme scores, it is an unreliable statistic. To get around this problem, we often use a modified version of the range—called the *interquartile range*. Since *inter-* means *between* and *-quartile* refers to *quarters, interquartile range* refers to the *range between quarters*. To find it, first divide the distribution into quarters, as shown in Figure 2. As you can see, the middle 50% of the subjects is between the values of 2.5 and 9.5. Since the formal definition of the *interquartile range (IQR)* is the *range of the middle 50% of the subjects*, we

can calculate it as follows: 9.5 − 2.5 = 7.0. Thus, *IQR* = 7.0.

1, 1, 1, 2, 3, 4, 5, 6, 7, 8, 8, 9, 10, 11, 11, 12
⇑                ⇑                ⇑
2.5            6.5            9.5

Figure 2  *Scores for Group A divided into quarters*

To see how the *IQR* helps us understand the variability in sets of data, let's consider Figure 3, where the median is 43.0 and the interquartile range is 71.0 (83.5 − 12.5 = 71.0)

0, 5, 7, 10, 15, 22, 30, 41, 45 , 57, 67, 78, 89, 92, 95, 99
⇑                    ⇑                    ⇑
12.5                43.0                83.5

Figure 3  *Scores for Group B divided into quarters*

Thus, for Groups A and B, we might find the data presented in a research report as illustrated in Table 1.

Table 1  *Medians and interquartile ranges for two groups*

| Group | Median | Interquartile Range |
|-------|--------|---------------------|
| A     | 6.5    | 7.0                 |
| B     | 43.0   | 71.0                |

As you can see, Table 1 indicates two things. First, Group A has a lower average than Group B (as indicated by the median of 6.5 for Group A vs. 43.0 for Group B). Second, Group A has less variability (as indicated by an interquartile range of 7.0 for Group A vs. 71.0 for Group B). Reconsideration of the scores shown in Figures 2 and 3 indicates that these results make sense. The middle score for Group A is much lower than the middle

---

[1]It is inappropriate to use the *mean* to describe ordinal data because the mean is the point around which the differences sum to zero. If the differences are unequal in size (as they would be with ordinal data), it makes no sense to use a statistic based on the differences. See Topics 39 and 44.

score for Group B, and the differences among the scores for Group A (1 vs. 1 vs. 1 vs. 1 vs. 2, etc.) are much smaller than the differences among the scores for Group B (0 vs. 5 vs. 7 vs. 10 vs. 15, etc.)—indicating less variability in Group A than Group B.

# Exercise on Topic 46

1. If the median for a group of subjects is 34.00, what percentage of the subjects has scores below a score of 34?

2. Should the mean *or* median be used with ordinal data?

3. How do you calculate the range of a set of scores?

4. Is the range *or* the interquartile range a more reliable statistic?

5. What is the definition of the *interquartile range*?

6. Suppose you read that for Group X, the median equals 55.1 and the *IQR* equals 30.0, while for Group Y, the median equals 62.9 and the *IQR* equals 25.0. Which group has the higher average score?

7. Based on the information in question 6, the scores for which group are more variable?

8. Which two statistics discussed in this topic are measures of variability?

9. Which two statistics mentioned in this topic are measures of central tendency (that is, are averages)?

## Question for Discussion

10. Name two circumstances under which the median is preferable to the mean.

## For Students Who Are Planning Research

11. Do you anticipate reporting medians and interquartile ranges? Explain.

# TOPIC 47 THE PEARSON CORRELATION COEFFICIENT

When we want to examine the relationship between two quantitative sets of scores (at the interval or ratio levels), we compute a correlation coefficient. The most widely used coefficient is the **Pearson product-moment correlation coefficient**, whose symbol is *r*. It is usually called simply **Pearson's *r***.

Consider again the scores in Table 1, which we considered in Topic 25. As you can see, the employment test scores put subjects in *roughly* the same order as the ratings by supervisors. In other words, those who had high employment test scores (such as Joe and Jane) tended to have high supervisors' ratings, *and* those who had low test scores (such as John and Jake) tended to have low

Table 1 *Direct relationship, r = .89*

| Employee | Employment Test Scores | Supervisors' Ratings |
|----------|-----------------------|----------------------|
| Joe | 35 | 9 |
| Jane | 32 | 10 |
| Bob | 29 | 8 |
| June | 27 | 8 |
| Leslie | 25 | 7 |
| Homer | 22 | 8 |
| Milly | 21 | 6 |
| Jake | 18 | 4 |
| John | 15 | 5 |

supervisors' ratings. This illustrates what we mean by a **direct relationship** (also called a **positive relationship**).

Note that the relationship in Table 1 is not perfect. For example, although Joe has a higher employment test score than Jane, Jane has a higher supervisor's rating than Joe. If the relationship were perfect, the value of the Pearson *r* would be 1.00. Being less than perfect, its actual

value is .89. As you can see in Figure 1, this value indicates a strong, direct relationship.

In an **inverse** relationship (also called a **negative relationship**), those who are high on

Table 2 *Inverse relationship, r = -.86*

| Employee | Self-Concept Scores | Depression Score |
|----------|---------------------|------------------|
| Joe | 10 | 2 |
| Jane | 8 | 1 |
| Bob | 9 | 0 |
| June | 7 | 5 |
| Leslie | 7 | 6 |
| Homer | 6 | 8 |
| Milly | 4 | 8 |
| Jake | 1 | 9 |
| John | 0 | 9 |

one variable are low on the other. Such a relationship exists between the scores in Table 2. Those who are high on self-concept (such as Joe and Jane) are low on depression while those who are low on self-concept (such as Jake and John) are high on depression. However, the relationship is not perfect. The value of the Pearson *r* for the relationship in Table 2 is -.86.

The relationships in Tables 1 and 2 are strong but, in each case, there are exceptions, which make the Pearson *r*s less than 1.00 and -.100. As the number and size of the exceptions increase, the values of the Pearson *r* become closer to 0.00. Therefore, a value of 0.00 indicates the complete absence of a relationship. (See Figure 1.)

It is important to note that a Pearson *r* is *not* a proportion and *cannot* be multiplied by 100 to get a percentage. For instance, a Pearson *r* of .50 does not correspond to 50% of anything. To think about correlation in terms of percentages, we must

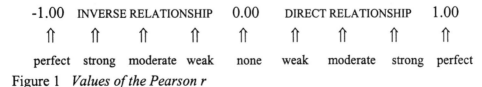

Figure 1 *Values of the Pearson r*

111

convert Pearson *r*s to another statistic, the **coefficient of determination**, whose symbol is $r^2$, which indicates how to compute it—simply square *r*. Thus, for an *r* of .50, $r^2$ equals .25. If we multiply .25 by 100, we get 25%. What does this mean? Simply this: A Pearson *r* of .50 is 25% better than a Pearson *r* of 0.00. Table 3 shows selected values of *r*, $r^2$, and the percentages you should think about when interpreting an *r*.[1]

Table 3   *Selected values of r and $r^2$*

| r | $r^2$ | Percentage better than zero[1] |
|---|---|---|
| .90 | .81 | 81% |
| .50 | .25 | 25% |
| .25 | .06 | 6% |
| -.25 | .06 | 6% |
| -.50 | .25 | 25% |
| -.90 | .81 | 81% |

[1]Also called *percentage of variance accounted for* or *percentage of explained variance.*

# EXERCISE ON TOPIC 47

1. "Pearson *r*" stands for what words?

2. When the relationship between two variables is perfect and inverse, what is the value of *r*?

3. Is it possible for a negative relationship to be strong?

4. Is an *r* of -.90 stronger than an *r* of .50?

5. Is a relationship direct or inverse when those with high scores on one variable have high scores on the other *and* those with low scores on one variable have low scores on the other?

6. What does an *r* of 1.00 indicate?

7. For a Pearson *r* of .60, what is the value of the coefficient of determination?

8. What do we do to a coefficient of determination to get a percentage?

9. A Pearson *r* of .70 is what percentage better than a Pearson *r* of 0.00?

## Question for Discussion

10. Name two variables between which you would expect to get a strong, positive value of *r*.

## For Students Who Are Planning Research

11. Will you be reporting Pearson *r*s? If so, name the two variables that will be correlated for each value of *r*.

---

[1]Note that the procedure for computing a Pearson *r* is beyond the scope of this book.

# TOPIC 48  THE *t* TEST

Suppose we have a *research hypothesis* that says "homicide investigators who take a short course on the causes of HIV will be less fearful of the disease than investigators who have not taken the course," and test it by conducting an experiment in which a random sample of investigators is assigned to take the course and another random sample is designated as the control group.[1] Let's suppose that at the end of the experiment the experimental group gets a mean of 16.61 on a fear of HIV scale and the control group gets a mean of 29.67 (where the higher the score, the greater the fear of HIV). These means support our research hypothesis. But can we be certain that our research hypothesis is correct? If you've been reading the topics on statistics in order from the beginning, you already know that the answer is "no" because of the **null hypothesis**, which says that there is no *true* difference between the means; that is, the difference was created merely by the chance errors created by random sampling. (These errors are known as *sampling errors*.) Put another way, unrepresentative groups may have been assigned to the two conditions quite at random.

The *t* test is often used to test the null hypothesis regarding the observed difference between two means.[2] For the example we are considering, a series of computations (which are beyond the scope of this book) would be performed to obtain a value of *t* (which, in this case, is 5.38) and a value of degrees of freedom (which, in this case, is $df = 179$). These values are not of any special interest to us except that they are used to get the *probability* (*p*) that the null hypothesis is true. In this particular case, *p* is less than .05. Thus, in a research report, you may read a statement such as this:

The difference between the means is statistically significant ($t = 5.38$, $df = 179$, $p < .05$).[3]

As you know from Topic 38, the term *statistically significant* indicates that the null hypothesis has been rejected. You should recall that when the probability that the null hypothesis is true is .05 or less (such as .01 or .001), we reject the null hypothesis. (When something is unlikely to be true because it has a low probability of being true, we reject it.)

Having rejected the null hypothesis, we are in a position to assert that our research hypothesis probably is true (assuming no procedural bias was allowed to affect the results, such as testing the control group immediately after a major news story on a famous person with AIDS, while testing the experimental group at an earlier time).

What leads a *t* test to give us a low probability? Three things:

1.  *Sample size.* The larger the sample, the less likely that an observed difference is due to sampling errors. (You should recall from the sections on sampling that larger samples provide more precise information.) Thus, when the sample is large, we are more likely to reject the null hypothesis than when the sample is small.

2.  *The size of the difference between means.* The larger the difference, the less likely that the difference is due to sampling errors. Thus, when the difference between the means is large, we are more likely to reject the null hypothesis than when the difference is small.

3.  *The amount of variation in the population.* You should recall from Topic 22 that when a population is very heterogeneous (has much variability) there is more potential for sampling error. Thus, when there is little variation (as indicated by the standard deviations of the sample), we are

---

[1]You probably recall that we prefer random sampling because it precludes any bias in the assignment of subjects to the groups and because we can test for the effect of random errors with significance tests; we cannot test for the effects of bias.

[2]To test the null hypothesis between two *medians*, the *median test* is used; it is a specialized form of the chi square test, whose results you already know how to interpret.

[3]Sometimes researchers leave out the abbreviation *df* and present the result as $t(179) = 5.38$, $p < .05$.

more likely to reject the null hypothesis than when there is much variation.

A special type of $t$ test is also applied to correlation coefficients. Suppose we drew a random sample of 50 students and correlated their hand size with their GPAs and got an $r$ of .19. The null hypothesis says that the *true* correlation in the population is 0.00—that we got .19 merely as the result of sampling errors. For this example, the $t$ test indicates that $p > .05$. Since the probability that the null hypothesis is true is greater than 5 in 100, we do *not* reject the null hypothesis; we have a statistically *in*significant correlation coefficient. (In other words, for $n = 50$, an $r$ of .19 is not significantly different from an $r$ of 0.00.) When reporting the results of the $t$ test for the significance of a correlation coefficient, it is conventional *not* to mention the value of $t$. Rather, researchers usually indicate only whether or not the correlation is significant at a given probability level.

# Exercise on Topic 48

1. What does the null hypothesis say about the difference between two sample means?

2. Is the value of $t$ usually of any special interest to consumers of research?

3. Suppose you read that for the difference between two means, $t = 2.000$, $df = 20$, $p > .05$. Using conventional standards, should you conclude that the null hypothesis should be rejected?

4. Suppose you read that for the difference between two means, $t = 2.859$, $df = 40$, $p < .01$. Using conventional standards, should you conclude that the null hypothesis should be rejected?

5. Based on the information in question 4, should you conclude that the difference between the means is statistically significant?

6. When we use a large sample, are we more *or* less likely to reject the null hypothesis than when we use a small sample?

7. When the size of the difference between means is large, are we more *or* less likely to reject the null hypothesis than when the size of the difference is small?

8. If we read that for a sample of 92 subjects, $r = .41$, $p < .001$, should we reject the null hypothesis?

9. Is the value of $r$ in question 8 statistically significant?

## Question for Discussion

10. Of the three things that lead to a low probability, which one is most directly under the control of a researcher?

## For Students Who Are Planning Research

11. Will you be conducting $t$ tests? Explain.

# TOPIC 49  ONE-WAY ANALYSIS OF VARIANCE

In the previous topic, you learned that the *t* test may be used to test the null hypothesis for the observed difference between two sample means.[1] An alternative test for this problem is **analysis of variance** (often called **ANOVA**).[2] Instead of *t*, it yields a statistic called *F*, as well as degrees of freedom (*df*), sum of squares, mean square, and a *p* value, which indicates the probability that the null hypothesis is correct. As with the *t* test, the only value of interest to the typical consumer of research is the value of *p*. By convention, when *p* equals .05 or less (such as .01 or .001), we reject the null hypothesis and declare the result to be *statistically significant*.

Because the *t* test and ANOVA are based on the same theory and assumptions, when we compare two means, both tests yield exactly the same value of *p* and, hence, lead to the same conclusion regarding significance. So for two means, both tests are equivalent. Note, however, that a single *t* test can compare only two means, but a single ANOVA can compare a number of means—which is a great advantage.

Suppose, for example, we try three drugs designed to treat depression in an experiment and obtain the means in Table 1.

Table 1   *Posttest means: Depression scores for three drugs*

| Drug A | Drug B | Drug C |
|--------|--------|--------|
| *M* = 6.00 | *M* = 5.50 | *M* = 2.33 |

Since the higher the score the greater the depression, inspection of the means shows that there are three observed differences:

(1) Drug C is superior to Drug A.
(2) Drug C is superior to Drug B.
(3) Drug B is superior to Drug A.

The null hypothesis says that this entire *set* of three differences was created by sampling error. Through a series of computations that are beyond

the scope of this book, an ANOVA for these data yields this result: $F = 10.837$, $df = 2, 15$, $p < .05$. This result might be stated in a sentence or presented in a table such as Table 2, which is known as an ANOVA table. While it contains many values, which were used to arrive at the probability, we are only interested in the end result—the value

Table 2   *ANOVA for data in Table 1*

| Source of Variation | df | Sum of Squares | Mean Square | F |
|---------------------|----|----------------|-------------|------|
| Between Groups | 2 | 47.445 | 23.722 | 10.837* |
| Within Groups | 15 | 32.833 | 2.189 | |
| Total | 17 | 80.278 | | |

*$p < .05$

of *p*. As you know, when the probability is .05 or less, as it is here, we reject the null hypothesis. This means that the *entire set* of differences is statistically significant at the .05 level. Note that the ANOVA does *not* tell us which of the three differences we listed are significant; it could be that only one, *or* only two, *or* all three are significant. This needs to be explored with additional tests, known as *multiple comparisons tests*. There are a number of such tests based on different assumptions—usually they yield the same result, but not always. For the data we are considering, application of a popular multiple comparisons test (Scheffé's test), yields these probabilities:

(1) for Drug C vs. A, $p < .05$
(2) for Drug C vs. B, $p < .05$
(3) for Drug B vs. A, $p > .05$

Thus, we have found that Drug C is significantly better than Drugs A and B, but that Drugs B and A are not significantly different from each other.

In review, an ANOVA tells us whether a set of differences, overall, is significant. If so, we can use a multiple comparisons test to determine which pair(s) of means are significantly different from each other.

---

[1]If you've been following along up to this point, you are already thoroughly familiar with the null hypothesis. If not, read Topics 38 and 48 before reading this one.
[2]Because it yields a value of *F*, it is sometimes called an *F test*.

In this topic, we have been considering a **one-way ANOVA** (also known as a **single-factor ANOVA**). It is called this because we have classified the subjects in only one way—in terms of which drug they took. In the next topic, we will consider the use of ANOVA when subjects are classified in two ways.

# EXERCISE ON TOPIC 49

1. ANOVA stands for what words?

2. If we compare two means for significance, will ANOVA and the *t* test yield the same probability?

3. If an ANOVA yields $p < .001$, should the null hypothesis be rejected?

4. If an ANOVA yields $p > .05$, are the difference(s) statistically significant?

5. If we have four means on an achievement test for samples of students in four states, can we determine whether the set of differences, overall, is statistically significant by using ANOVA?

6. For the information in question 5, could we use a *t* test for the same purpose?

7. Should the typical consumer of research be concerned with the values of the sum of squares?

8. In an ANOVA table, which statistic is of the greatest interest to the typical consumer of research?

9. If an overall ANOVA for three or more means is significant, it can be followed up with what type of test to determine the significance of the differences among the individual pairs of means?

## Questions for Discussion

10. Very briefly describe a hypothetical study in which it would be appropriate to conduct a one-way ANOVA but it would *not* be appropriate to conduct a *t* test.

11. If you have means for four groups, you have how many individual pairs of means to be compared with a multiple comparisons test?

## For Students Who Are Planning Research

12. Will you be conducting a one-way ANOVA? Explain.

# TOPIC 50 TWO-WAY ANALYSIS OF VARIANCE

In the previous topic, we saw how **ANOVA** can be used to test for the overall significance of a set of means when subjects have been classified in one way. Often, however, it is desirable to look at a two-way classification such as (1) which drug was taken and (2) how long subjects have been depressed. Table 1 shows the means for such a study.[1] Since higher depression scores indicate more depression, a low mean is desirable.

Table 1 *Means for a study of depression: Drugs and length of depression comparisons*

|  | Drug A | Drug B | Row Total |
|---|---|---|---|
| Long-term | $M = 8.11$ | $M = 8.32$ | **$M = 8.22$** |
| Short-term | $M = 4.67$ | $M = 8.45$ | **$M = 6.56$** |
| **Col. Total** | **$M = 6.39$** | **$M = 8.38$** | |

Although the subjects are classified in two ways, analysis of the table answers *three* questions. First by comparing the column totals of 6.39 and 8.38, we can see that, overall, those who took Drug A are less depressed. It's important to notice that the mean of 6.39 for Drug A is based on both those who have long-term *and* those who have short-term depression; the same is true of the mean of 8.38 for Drug B. Thus, by comparing the column total means, we are answering the question of which drug is more effective *in general without regard to how long subjects have been depressed*. In analysis of variance, this is known as a **main effect**.

Each way in which subjects are classified yields a main effect in analysis of variance. Thus, since subjects were also classified in terms of their length of depression, there is a main effect for short-term vs. long-term, which can be seen by examining the row total means of 8.22 and 6.56. This main effect indicates that, overall, those with short-term depression are less depressed than those with long-term depression.

In this example, the most interesting question is the question of an **interaction**. The question is

simply this: "Is the effectiveness of the drugs dependent, in part, on the length of depression?" By examining the individual cell means (those *not* in bold in Table 1), we can see that the answer is "yes." Drug A is more effective for short-term than long-term depression (4.67 vs. 8.11) while Drug B is about equally effective for both types of depression (8.32 vs. 8.45). What is the practical implication of this interaction? The overall effectiveness of Drug A is almost entirely attributable to its effectiveness for short-term depression. That is, if a person has short-term depression, Drug A is indicated, but if a person has long-term depression, either drug is likely to be about equally effective.

For the data in Table 1, it turns out that $p < .05$ for both main effects and the interaction. Thus, we can reject the null hypotheses that say that the differences we are considering are the result of random errors. Of course, it does not always turn out this way—it's possible for one or two of the main effects to be significant but the interaction to be not significant; it's also possible for neither main effect to be significant while the interaction is significant, which is the case for the data in Table 2.

Table 2 *Means for a study of depression: Drugs and gender comparisons*

|  | Drug A | Drug B | Row Total |
|---|---|---|---|
| Females | $M = 8.00$ | $M = 5.00$ | **$M = 6.50$** |
| Males | $M = 5.00$ | $M = 8.00$ | **$M = 6.50$** |
| **Col. Total** | **$M = 6.50$** | **$M = 6.50$** | |

Notice that the column totals (6.50 vs. 6.50) in Table 2 indicate no main effect for Drug A vs. Drug B. Likewise, the row totals (6.50 vs. 6.50) indicate no main effect for gender. But there is a very interesting finding—the *interaction* of drug type and gender, which indicates that for females, Drug B is superior, but for males, Drug A is superior. Note that if we had compared the two drugs

---

[1]For instructional purposes, only two types of drugs are shown. However, we may use ANOVA when there are more than two.

in a one-way ANOVA without also classifying the subjects according to gender (as we did here in a two-way ANOVA), we would have missed this important interaction.

# EXERCISE ON TOPIC 50

1. Suppose we drew random samples of urban, suburban, and rural children, tested them for creativity, and obtained three means. Should we use a one-way or two-way ANOVA to test for significance?

2. Do the following means on a performance test indicate an interaction between type of reward and age?

|  | Praise Reward | Monetary Reward | Row Total |
|---|---|---|---|
| Young Adults | $M = 50.00$ | $M = 60.00$ | $M = 55.00$ |
| Older Adults | $M = 60.00$ | $M = 50.00$ | $M = 55.00$ |
| Col. Total | $M = 55.00$ | $M = 55.00$ | |

3. Do the means for question 2 indicate a main effect for type of reward?

4. Do the following means on an achievement test indicate an interaction between the method of instruction (A vs. B) and the aptitude of the students (high vs. low)?

|  | Method A | Method B | Row Total |
|---|---|---|---|
| High Aptitude | $M = 100.00$ | $M = 85.00$ | $M = 92.50$ |
| Low Aptitude | $M = 100.00$ | $M = 85.00$ | $M = 92.50$ |
| Col. Total | $M = 100.00$ | $M = 85.00$ | |

5. Do the means for question 4 indicate a main effect for method of instruction?

6. Do the means for question 4 indicate a main effect for aptitude?

7. If $p > .05$ for an interaction in an analysis of variance, should we reject the null hypothesis?

## Question for Discussion

8. Very briefly describe a hypothetical study in which it would be appropriate to conduct a two-way ANOVA but it would *not* be appropriate to conduct a one-way ANOVA.

## For Students Who Are Planning Research

9. Will you be conducting a two-way ANOVA? Explain.

# TOPIC 51  PRACTICAL SIGNIFICANCE OF RESULTS

As you know from previous topics, *statistical significance* tells us whether a difference is reliable in light of random errors. Assume, for example, that we assigned students at random to two groups: one that learned a particular math lesson using new instructional software (the experimental group) and one that learned using a traditional lecture/textbook approach (the control group). Let us assume, furthermore, that use of the instructional software *in truth* is very slightly superior to the lecture/textbook approach (i.e., it really produces a superior outcome, but the superiority is quite small). With a very large sample, randomization should give us experimental and control groups that are very similar at the onset of the experiment (i.e., on the pretest). Since larger samples have less sampling error, a significance test such as a *t* test for the difference between the two posttest means may be able to detect the reliability of this small difference and allow us to declare it to be *statistically significant* at some probability level such as $p < .05$. Thus, we arrive at an important point: Even a small difference can be a statistically significant difference.[1]

While determining the statistical significance of a difference is the first step, determining the *practical significance* is the next step. Determining practical significance involves four considerations.

The first is the cost in relation to the benefit, which is often referred to as a *cost-benefit analysis*. While there are mechanical, statistical means for conducting such an analysis, for most purposes, common sense and good judgment can give us a good answer to the question of whether the results are of practical significance in terms of cost. Consider the example we started with above. Suppose that all students already have access to computers for their math lessons and that the software is being donated (or is highly subsidized by some foundation). In this case, the low cost might make the small difference practically significant. On the other hand, if expensive computers and

software would need to be purchased and the teachers would need extensive (and, therefore, expensive) training in its use, we might forgo using the experimental method in everyday instruction if we were going to obtain only a very small increase in math performance.

As you have just seen, even a small difference can be of both statistical and practical significance if the cost is low. In addition, a small, statistically significant difference can be of practical significance—even if it is costly—if it is a *crucial difference*. A crucial difference is one that makes a very important difference. Consider an extreme example. Suppose an experiment in which very expensive computerized simulations that teach how to conduct a delicate form of surgery reduces the death rate from such surgery from 2 in 100,000 to 1 in 100,000. We might well decide that even this small difference is worth the high cost because saving lives during surgery is crucial. A less extreme example is if a school needs just a few points increase (on the average) to cross a crucial threshold such as having the average student score at or above the 50th percentile rank on a standardized math test. Crossing that threshold might be considered crucial if it means that the school will be regarded by the public as better than other schools and if teachers will receive additional compensation in their salaries for bringing their school up to par (on the average).

The second consideration in determining practical significance is *client acceptability*. In school settings, students are clients. If a statistically superior computerized approach is greatly disliked by them (perhaps causing classroom control problems and the development of negative attitudes toward math), then the statistically significant difference might be of little practical significance.

The third consideration is *public and political acceptability*. For example, studies suggest that stem cell research might be fruitful in curing a number of debilitating and deadly diseases. Yet,

---

[1]As you know from Topic 48, the *t* test is more likely to lead to significance if the difference between the two means is large. However, if there is little variation among the participants and if a large enough sample is used, even small reliable differences can be detected and declared statistically significant.

large segments of the public (at the time of this writing) are opposed to it, calling into question its practical significance as a line of research that scientists should continue to pursue.

Fourth, we need to consider the *ethical and legal* implications of a statistically significant result. However much benefit and no matter how low the cost, some treatments that have been shown to produce statistically superior results may violate the ethical standards of a profession or impinge on legal requirements such as the many laws that govern the operation of the schools or deny clients the full protection of their rights spelled out in the Constitution as well as local and national laws.

As you can see, determining practical significance cannot be done mechanically. If there is any question as to the practical significance of the results of a study, representative groups of potential providers of the treatments such as teachers or psychologists, their clients, the public, and politicians may need to be consulted. In addition legal counsel may be needed.

In the next topic, you will learn about a statistical method that helps us determine whether a difference is large.

# EXERCISE ON TOPIC 51

1. Is it possible for a small difference to be statistically significant?

2. This topic describes how many types of considerations involved in determining practical significance?

3. If the cost is very low, might a very small statistically significant difference be of practical significance?

4. A crucial difference might make a very small statistically significant difference of practical significance. Is this statement true or false?

5. According to this topic, should the acceptability of a treatment to the clients be considered when determining practical significance?

6. According to this topic, ethical considerations should play no role in the interpretation of the results of a study. Is this statement true or false?

7. Is the determination of the practical significance of the results of a study a mechanical process?

## Questions for Discussion

8. In addition to the two examples in this topic, name a hypothetical result that might make a *crucial difference* that you would favor implementing even if it were costly.

9. Consider the last article you read that had statistically significant results. Did the researcher who wrote the article discuss the practical significance of his or her results? Explain.

## For Students Who Are Planning Research

10. Can you anticipate any considerations that might limit the practical significance of your results?

# TOPIC 52  INTRODUCTION TO EFFECT SIZE

To understand the need to consider the *effect size* of a difference, let us consider a practical problem in interpreting research. Suppose that two researchers conducted well-designed and rigorously controlled experiments with depression as the dependent variable. Suppose that Experimenter A used Treatment X for the experimental group while Experimenter B used Treatment Y for the experimental group. Both experimenters randomly assigned participants to experimental and control conditions. Suppose Experimenter A used a 20-item true-false depression scale (with possible raw scores[1] from 0 to 20), and obtained the result on the posttest shown in Table 1.[2]

Table 1   *Statistics obtained by Experimenter A*

| Group | M | SD |
|---|---|---|
| Experimental group (*n* = 50) | 12.0 | 2.3 |
| Control group (*n* = 50) | 7.0 | 2.0 |
| Difference between means | 5.0* | |

*\*p < .05*

Furthermore, suppose Experimenter B use a 30-item scale with choices from Strongly Agree to Strongly disagree with possible raw scores from 0 to 120 and obtained the results in Table 2.

Table 2   *Statistics obtained by Experimenter B*

| Group | M | SD |
|---|---|---|
| Experimental group (*n* = 50) | 80.0 | 14.5 |
| Control group (*n* = 50) | 70.0 | 15.0 |
| Difference between means | 10.0* | |

*\*p < .05*

So which treatment is superior? The one used by Experimenter A, with a 5-point difference between the means *or* the one used by Experimenter B, with a 10-point difference between the means?

Of course, the answer is not immediately clear because the two experimenters used different scales (0 to 20 versus 0 to 120). The solution is to standardize the results by calculating the *effect size* for each experiment. To calculate it, we use the means and standard deviations. Notice that Experimenter A has smaller means, a smaller mean difference, and smaller standard deviations, which is realistic given that the scores could range from only 0 to 20. Experimenter B has larger statistics on all three counts. The calculation of effect size (whose symbol is $d$) adjusts for these differences by interpreting the difference between the means in terms of the standard deviations. For Experimenter A, we first subtract the control group mean from the experimental group mean, which we know results in a difference of 5. Then we divide this difference by the standard deviation of the control group, that is, 5 divided by 2.0 equals 2.5. Thus, 2.5 is the effect size for Experimenter A. What does 2.5 mean? It means that the experimental group exceeded the control group by 2.5 standard deviation units. (You might want to review Topic 45 to refresh your memory regarding the meaning of the standard deviation.)[3]

Doing the same thing for Experimenter B's results, we divide the difference between the means (10.0) by the control group's standard deviation of 15.0 and obtain this effect size: $d = .67$.

Remember that $d$ tells us by how many standard deviations the experimental group exceeded the control group. Since we have calculated $d$ for both experiments, we now know that when the results are standardized, Experimenter A's results (with a $d$ of 2.5) are much stronger than Experimenter B's results (with a $d$ of .67). Keeping in mind that there are only about three standard deviation units on both sides of the mean, a $d$ of 2.5 on the positive side is quite impressive.

Many statisticians encourage researchers to

[1]Raw scores are the number of points earned or awarded before any conversion such as a conversion to percentile ranks, standard scores, or grade equivalents.

[2]Note that in both tables, *higher* mean scores indicate *less* depression.

[3]Some researchers divide the difference between the means by the "pooled standard deviation" instead of the standard deviation of the control group. The pooled standard deviation is a special type of average of the standard deviations of the experimental and control groups.

report their effect size(s) even if they are not comparing two or more studies. For example, Experimenter A might report her effect size of 2.5 even if Experimenter B had not conducted his study. Seeing an effect size of 2.5, a reader who knows that the effective range of standard deviation units is only from –3.0 to +3.0 would be impressed by the magnitude of the difference (which might be lost on a reader who saw only a difference of 5 raw score points between Experimenter A's two means).

Unfortunately, there are no uniform standards for interpreting effect size. However, when $d$ is .30 or more, it is usually regarded as being reasonably strong. Both of the experimenters in our example greatly exceeded this threshold.[4]

# EXERCISE ON TOPIC 52

1. In this topic, did Experimenter A *or* Experimenter B have a larger mean score difference?

2. In this topic, did Experimenter A *or* Experimenter B have a larger effect size?

3. In this topic, the effect sizes were standardized because the raw score differences between the means were divided by what statistic?

4. Suppose you conducted an experiment on improving algebra achievement and your experimental post-test mean equaled 500.0 ($sd = 100.0$) and your control group mean equaled 400 ($sd = 100$). What is the value of the effect size for your experiment?

5. Suppose an effect size equals 2.9. According to this topic, would this be impressively large?

6. Would a $d$ of .15 be considered reasonably large?

7. Would a $d$ of .35 be considered reasonably large?

## Question for Discussion

8. Some researchers have strongly urged all researchers to report effect sizes (when possible) in their reports of their research. Do you think this is a good idea? Would it help you understand research reports? Explain.

## For Students Who Are Planning Research

9. Do you plan to report the effect size(s) for your study? Explain.

---

[4]See Appendix G for information on how effect sizes can be used to combine and summarize the results of various studies through the application of a technique called meta-analysis.

# Appendix A

# Examining the Validity Structure of Qualitative Research

R. BURKE JOHNSON
University of South Alabama

ABSTRACT. Three types of validity in qualitative research are discussed. First, descriptive validity refers to the factual accuracy of the account as reported by the qualitative researcher. Second, interpretive validity is obtained to the degree that the participants' viewpoints, thoughts, intentions, and experiences are accurately understood and reported by the qualitative researcher. Third, theoretical validity is obtained to the degree that a theory or theoretical explanation developed from a research study fits the data and is, therefore, credible and defensible. The two types of validity that are typical of quantitative research, internal and external validity, are also discussed for qualitative research. Twelve strategies used to promote research validity in qualitative research are discussed.

From Education, 118, 282–292. Copyright © 1997 by Project Innovation. Reprinted with permission of the publisher and author.

Discussions of the term "validity" have traditionally been attached to the quantitative research tradition. Not surprisingly, reactions by qualitative researchers have been mixed regarding whether or not this concept should be applied to qualitative research. At the extreme, some qualitative researchers have suggested that the traditional quantitative criteria of reliability and validity are not relevant to qualitative research (e.g., Smith, 1984). Smith contends that the basic epistemological and ontological assumptions of quantitative and qualitative research are incompatible, and, therefore, the concepts of reliability and validity should be abandoned. Most qualitative researchers, however, probably hold a more moderate viewpoint. Most qualitative researchers argue that some qualitative research studies are better than others, and they frequently use the term validity to refer to this difference. When qualitative researchers speak of research validity, they are usually referring to qualitative research that is plausible, credible, trustworthy, and, therefore, defensible. We believe it is important to think about the issue of validity in qualitative research and to examine some strategies that have been developed to maximize validity (Kirk & Miller, 1986; LeCompte & Preissle, 1993; Lincoln & Guba, 1985; Maxwell, 1996). A list of these strategies is provided in Table 1.

One potential threat to validity that researchers must be careful to watch out for is called *researcher bias*. This problem is summed up in a statement a colleague of mine once made to me. She said, "The problem with qualitative research is that the researchers find what they want to find, and then they write up their results." It is true that the problem of researcher bias is frequently an issue because qualitative research is open-ended and less structured than quantitative research. This is because qualitative research tends to be exploratory. (One would be remiss, however, to think that researcher bias is never a problem in quantitative research!) Researcher bias tends to result from selective observation and selective recording of information, and also from allowing one's personal views and perspectives to affect how data are interpreted and how the research is conducted.

The key strategy used to understand researcher bias is called *reflexivity*, which means that the researcher actively engages in critical self-reflection about his or her potential biases and predispositions (Table 1). Through reflexivity, researchers become more self-aware, and they monitor and attempt to control their biases. Many qualitative researchers include a distinct section in their research proposals titled Researcher Bias. In this section, they discuss their personal background, how it may affect their research, and what strategies they will use to address the potential problem. Another strategy that qualitative researchers use to reduce the effect of researcher bias is called *negative case sampling* (Table 1). This means that they attempt carefully and purposively to search for examples that disconfirm their expectations and explanations about what they are studying. If you use this approach, you will find it more difficult to ignore important information, and you will come up with more credible and defensible results.

We will now examine some types of validity that are important in qualitative research. We will start with three types of validity that are especially relevant to qualitative research (Maxwell, 1992, 1996). These types are called descriptive validity, interpretive validity, and theoretical validity. They are important to qualitative research because description of what is ob-

Table 1
Strategies Used to Promote Qualitative Research Validity

| Strategy | Description |
|---|---|
| Researcher as "Detective" | A metaphor characterizing the qualitative researcher as he or she searches for evidence about causes and effects. The researcher develops an understanding of the data through careful consideration of potential causes and effects and by systematically eliminating "rival" explanations or hypotheses until the final "case" is made "beyond a reasonable doubt." The "detective" can utilize any of the strategies listed here. |
| Extended fieldwork | When possible, qualitative researchers should collect data in the field over an extended period of time. |
| Low inference descriptors | The use of description phrased very close to the participants' accounts and researchers' field notes. Verbatims (i.e., direct quotations) are a commonly used type of low inference descriptors. |
| Triangulation | "Cross-checking" information and conclusions through the use of multiple procedures or sources. When the different procedures or sources are in agreement, you have "corroboration." |
| Data triangulation | The use of multiple data sources to help understand a phenomenon. |
| Methods triangulation | The use of multiple research methods to study a phenomenon. |
| Investigator triangulation | The use of multiple investigators (i.e., multiple researchers) in collecting and interpreting the data. |
| Theory triangulation | The use of multiple theories and perspectives to help interpret and explain the data. |
| Participant feedback | The feedback and discussion of the researcher's interpretations and conclusions with the actual participants and other members of the participant community for verification and insight. |
| Peer review | Discussion of the researcher's interpretations and conclusions with other people. This includes discussion with a "disinterested peer" (e.g., with another researcher not directly involved). This peer should be skeptical and play the "devil's advocate," challenging the researcher to provide solid evidence for any interpretations or conclusions. Discussion with peers who are familiar with the research can also help provide useful challenges and insights. |
| Negative case sampling | Locating and examining cases that disconfirm the researcher's expectations and tentative explanation. |
| Reflexivity | This involves self-awareness and "critical self-reflection" by the researcher on his or her potential biases and predispositions as these may affect the research process and conclusions. |
| Pattern matching | Predicting a series of results that form a "pattern" and then determining the degree to which the actual results fit the predicted pattern. |

served and interpretation of participants' thoughts are two primary qualitative research activities. For example, ethnography produces descriptions and accounts of the lives and experiences of groups of people with a focus on cultural characteristics (Fetterman, 1998; LeCompte & Preissle, 1993). Ethnographers also attempt to understand groups of people from the insider's perspective (i.e., from the viewpoints of the people in the group; called the *emic* perspective). Developing a theoretical explanation of the behavior of group members is also of interest to qualitative researchers, especially qualitative researchers using the grounded theory perspective (Glaser & Strauss, 1967; Strauss and Corbin, 1990). After discussing these three forms of validity, the traditional types of validity used in quantitative research, internal and external validity, are discussed. Internal validity is relevant when qualitative researchers explore cause and effect relationships. External validity is relevant when qualitative researchers generalize beyond their research studies.

### Descriptive Validity

The first type of validity in qualitative research is called *descriptive validity*. Descriptive validity refers to the factual accuracy of the account as reported by the researchers. The key questions addressed in descriptive validity are: Did what was reported as taking place in the group being studied actually happen? and Did the researchers accurately report what they saw and heard? In other words, descriptive validity refers to accuracy in reporting descriptive information (e.g., description of events, objects, behaviors, people, settings, times, and places). This form of validity is important because description is a major objective in nearly all qualitative research.

One effective strategy used to obtain descriptive validity is called *investigator triangulation*. In the case of descriptive validity, investigator triangulation involves the use of multiple observers to record and describe the research participants' behavior and the context in which they were located. The use of multiple observers allows cross-checking of observations to make sure the investigators agree about what took place. When corroboration (i.e., agreement) of observations across multiple investigators is obtained, it is less likely that outside reviewers of the research will question whether something occurred. As a result, the research will be more credible and defensible.

## Interpretive Validity

While descriptive validity refers to accuracy in reporting the facts, interpretive validity requires developing a window into the minds of the people being studied. *Interpretive validity* refers to accurately portraying the *meaning* attached by participants to what is being studied by the researcher. More specifically, it refers to the degree to which the research participants' viewpoints, thoughts, feelings, intentions, and experiences are accurately understood by the qualitative researcher and portrayed in the research report. An important part of qualitative research is understanding research participants' inner worlds (i.e., their phenomenological worlds), and interpretive validity refers to the degree of accuracy in presenting these inner worlds. Accurate interpretive validity requires that the researcher get inside the heads of the participants, look through the participants' eyes, and see and feel what they see and feel. In this way, the qualitative researcher can understand things from the participants' perspectives and provide a valid account of these perspectives.

Some strategies for achieving interpretive validity are provided in Table 1. *Participant feedback* is perhaps the most important strategy (Table 1). This strategy has also been called "member checking" (Lincoln & Guba, 1985). By sharing your interpretations of participants' viewpoints with the participants and other members of the group, you may clear up areas of miscommunication. Do the people being studied agree with what you have said about them? While this strategy is not perfect, because some participants may attempt to put on a good face, useful information is frequently obtained and inaccuracies are often identified.

When writing the research report, using many low inference descriptors is also helpful so that the reader can experience the participants' actual language, dialect, and personal meanings (Table 1). A verbatim is the lowest inference descriptor of all because the participants' exact words are provided in direct quotations. Here is an example of a verbatim from a high school dropout who was part of an ethnographic study of high school dropouts:

I wouldn't do the work. I didn't like the teacher and I didn't like my mom and dad. So, even if I did my work, I wouldn't turn it in. I completed it. I just didn't want to

turn it in. I was angry with my mom and dad because they were talking about moving out of state at the time (Okey & Cusick, 1995: p. 257).

This verbatim provides some description (i.e., what the participant did) but it also provides some information about the participant's interpretations and personal meanings (which is the topic of interpretive validity). The participant expresses his frustration and anger toward his parents and teacher, and shares with us what homework meant to him at the time and why he acted as he did. By reading verbatims like this one, readers of a report can experience for themselves the participants' perspectives. Again, getting into the minds of research participants is a common goal in qualitative research, and Maxwell calls our accuracy in portraying this inner content interpretive validity.

## Theoretical Validity

The third type of validity in qualitative research is called *theoretical validity*. You have theoretical validity to the degree that a theoretical explanation developed from a research study fits the data and, therefore, is credible and defensible. Theory usually refers to discussions of *how* a phenomenon operates and *why* it operates as it does. Theory is usually more abstract and less concrete than description and interpretation. Theory development moves beyond just the facts and provides an explanation of the phenomenon. In the words of Joseph Maxwell (1992):

...one could label the student's throwing of the eraser as an act of resistance, and connect this act to the repressive behavior or values of the teacher, the social structure of the school, and class relationships in U.S. society. The identification of the throwing as resistance constitutes the application of a theoretical construct...the connection of this to other aspects of the participants, the school, or the community constitutes the postulation of theoretical relationships among these constructs (p. 291).

In the above example, the theoretical construct called "resistance" is used to explain the student's behavior. Maxwell points out that the construct of resistance may also be related to other theoretical constructs or variables. In fact, theories are often developed by relating theoretical constructs.

A strategy for promoting theoretical validity is *extended fieldwork* (Table 1). This means that you should spend a sufficient amount of time studying your research participants and their setting so that you can have confidence that the patterns of relationships you believe are operating are stable and so that you can understand why these relationships occur. As you spend more time in the field collecting data and generating and testing your inductive hypotheses, your theoretical explanation may become more detailed and intricate. You may also decide to use the strategy called *theory triangulation* (Table 1; Denzin, 1989). This means that you would examine how the phenomenon being studied would be explained by different theories.

The various theories might provide you with insights and help you develop a more cogent explanation. In a related way, you might also use investigator triangulation and consider the ideas and explanations generated by additional researchers studying the research participants.

As you develop your theoretical explanation, you should make some predictions based on the theory and test the accuracy of those predictions. When doing this, you can use the *pattern matching* strategy (Table 1). In pattern matching, the strategy is to make several predictions at once; then, if all of the predictions occur as predicted (i.e., if the pattern is found), you have evidence supporting your explanation. As you develop your theoretical explanation, you should also use the negative case sampling strategy mentioned earlier (Table 1). That is, you must always search for cases or examples that do not fit your explanation so that you do not simply find the data that support your developing theory. As a general rule, your final explanation should accurately reflect the majority of the people in your research study. Another useful strategy for promoting theoretical validity is called *peer review* (Table 1). This means that you should try to spend some time discussing your explanation with your colleagues so that they can search for problems with it. Each problem must then be resolved. In some cases, you will find that you will need to go back to the field and collect additional data. Finally, when developing a theoretical explanation, you must also think about the issues of internal validity and external validity to which we now turn.

## Internal Validity

Internal validity is the fourth type of validity in qualitative research of interest to us. Internal validity refers to the degree to which a researcher is justified in concluding that an observed relationship is causal (Cook and Campbell, 1979). Often, qualitative researchers are not interested in cause and effect relationships. Sometimes, however, qualitative researchers are interested in identifying potential causes and effects. In fact, qualitative research can be very helpful in describing how phenomena operate (i.e., studying process) and in developing and testing preliminary causal hypotheses and theories (Campbell, 1979; Johnson, 1994; LeCompte & Preissle, 1993; Strauss, 1995; 1994).

When qualitative researchers identify potential cause and effect relationships, they must think about many of the same issues that quantitative researchers must consider. They should also think about the strategies used for obtaining theoretical validity discussed earlier. The qualitative researcher takes on the role of the detective searching for the true cause(s) of a phenomenon, examining each possible clue, and attempting to rule out each rival explanation generated (see *Researcher as "Detective"* in Table 1). When trying to identify a causal relationship, the researcher makes

mental comparisons. The comparison might be to a hypothetical control group. Although a control group is rarely used in qualitative research, the researcher can think about what would have happened if the causal factor had not occurred. The researcher can sometimes rely on his or her expert opinion, as well as published research studies when available, in deciding what would have happened. Furthermore, if the event is something that occurs again, the researcher can determine if the causal factor precedes the outcome. In other words, when the causal factor occurs again, does the effect follow?

When a researcher believes that an observed relationship is causal, he or she must also attempt to make sure that the observed change in the dependent variable is due to the independent variable and not to something else (e.g., a confounding extraneous variable). The successful researcher will always make a list of rival explanations or rival hypotheses, which are possible or plausible reasons for the relationship other than the originally suspected cause. Be creative and think of as many rival explanations as you can. One way to get started is to be a skeptic and think of reasons why the relationship should not be causal. Each rival explanation must be examined after the list has been developed. Sometimes you will be able to check a rival explanation with the data you have already collected through additional data analysis. At other times you will need to collect additional data. One strategy would be to observe the relationship you believe to be causal under conditions where the confounding variable is not present and compare this outcome with the original outcome. For example, if you concluded that a teacher effectively maintained classroom discipline on a given day but a critic maintained that it was the result of a parent visiting the classroom on that day, then you should try to observe the teacher again when the parent is not present. If the teacher is still successful, you have some evidence that the original finding was not because of the presence of the parent in the classroom.

All of the strategies shown in Table 1 are used to improve the internal validity of qualitative research. Now we will explain the only two strategies not yet discussed (i.e., methods triangulation and data triangulation). When using *methods triangulation*, the researcher uses more than one method of research in a single research study. The word methods should be used broadly here, and it refers to different methods of research (e.g., ethnography, survey, experimental, etc.) as well as to different types of data collection procedures (e.g., interviews, questionnaires, and observations). You can intermix any of these (e.g., ethnography and survey research methods, or interviews and observations, or experimental research and interviews). The logic is to combine different methods that have "nonoverlapping weaknesses and strengths" (Brewer & Hunter, 1989). The weaknesses (and strengths) of one method will tend to be different from those of a different method, which means that when you combine two or more methods you will have better evidence! In other words, the "whole" is better than its "parts."

Here is an example of methods triangulation. Perhaps you are interested in why students in an elementary classroom stigmatize a certain student named Brian. A stigmatized student would be an individual that is not well liked, has a lower status, and is seen as different from the normal students. Perhaps Brian has a different haircut from the other students, is dressed differently, or doesn't act like the other students. In this case, you might decide to observe how students treat Brian in various situations. In addition to observing the students, you will probably decide to interview Brian and the other students to understand their beliefs and feelings about Brian. A strength of observational data is that you can actually see the students' behaviors. A weakness of interviews is that what the students say and what they actually do may be different. However, using interviews you can delve into the students' thinking and reasoning, whereas you cannot do this using observational data. Therefore, the whole will likely be better than the parts.

When using *data triangulation*, the researcher uses multiple data sources in a single research study. "Data sources" does not mean using different methods. Data triangulation refers to the use of multiple data sources using a single method. For example, the use of multiple interviews would provide multiple data sources while using a single method (i.e., the interview method). Likewise, the use of multiple observations would be another example of data triangulation; multiple data sources would be provided while using a single method (i.e., the observational method). Another important part of data triangulation involves collecting data at different times, at different places, and with different people.

Here is an example of data triangulation. Perhaps a researcher is interested in studying why certain students are apathetic. It would make sense to get the perspectives of several different kinds of people. The researcher might interview teachers, interview students identified by the teachers as being apathetic, and interview peers of apathetic students. Then the researcher could check to see if the information obtained from these different data sources was in agreement. Each data source may provide additional reasons as well as a different perspective on the question of student apathy, resulting in a more complete understanding of the phenomenon. The researcher should also interview apathetic students at different class periods during the day and in different types of classes (e.g., math and social studies). Through the rich information gathered (e.g., from different people, at different times, and at different places) the researcher can develop a better understanding of why students are apathetic than if only one data source is used.

## External Validity

External validity is important when you want to generalize from a set of research findings to other people, settings, and times (Cook and Campbell, 1979). Typically, generalizability is not the major purpose of qualitative research. There are at least two reasons for this. First, the people and settings examined in qualitative research are rarely randomly selected, and, as you know, random selection is the best way to generalize from a sample to a population. As a result, qualitative research is virtually always weak in the form of population validity focused on "generalizing to populations" (i.e., generalizing from a sample to a population).

Second, some qualitative researchers are more interested in documenting particularistic findings than universalistic findings. In other words, in certain forms of qualitative research the goal is to show what is unique about a certain group of people, or a certain event, rather than generate findings that are broadly applicable. At a fundamental level, many qualitative researchers do not believe in the presence of general laws or universal laws. General laws are things that apply to many people, and universal laws are things that apply to everyone. As a result, qualitative research is frequently considered weak on the "generalizing across populations" form of population validity (i.e., generalizing to different kinds of people), and on ecological validity (i.e., generalizing across settings) and temporal validity (i.e., generalizing across times).

Other experts argue that rough generalizations can be made from qualitative research. Perhaps the most reasonable stance toward the issue of generalizing is that we can generalize to other people, settings, and times to the degree that they are similar to the people, settings, and times in the original study. Stake (1990) uses the term *naturalistic generalization[1]* to refer to this process of generalizing based on similarity. The bottom line is this: The more similar the people and circumstances in a particular research study are to the ones that you want to generalize to, the more defensible your generalization will be and the more readily you should make such a generalization.

To help readers of a research report know when they can generalize, qualitative researchers should provide the following kinds of information: the number and kinds of people in the study, how they were selected to be in the study, contextual information, the nature of the researcher's relationship with the participants, information about any informants who provided information, the methods of data collection used, and

---

[1] Donald Campbell (1986) makes a similar point, and he uses the term *proximal similarity* to refer to the degree of similarity between the people and circumstances in the original research study and the people and circumstances to which you wish to apply the findings. Using Campbell's term, your goal is to check for proximal similarity.

the data analysis techniques used. This information is usually reported in the Methodology section of the final research report. Using the information included in a well-written methodology section, readers will be able to make informed decisions about to whom the results may be generalized. They will also have the information they will need if they decide to replicate the research study with new participants.

Some experts show another way to generalize from qualitative research (e.g., Yin, 1994). Qualitative researchers can sometimes use *replication logic,* just like the replication logic that is commonly used by experimental researchers when they generalize beyond the people in their studies, even when they do not have random samples. According to replication logic, the more times a research finding is shown to be true with different sets of people, the more confidence we can place in the finding and in the conclusion that the finding generalizes beyond the people in the original research study (Cook and Campbell, 1979). In other words, if the finding is replicated with different kinds of people and in different places, then the evidence may suggest that the finding applies very broadly. Yin's key point is that there is no reason why replication logic cannot be applied to certain kinds of qualitative research.[2]

Here is an example. Over the years you may observe a certain pattern of relations between boys and girls in your third-grade classroom. Now assume that you decided to conduct a qualitative research study and you find that the pattern of relation occurred in your classroom and in two other third-grade classrooms you studied. Because your research is interesting, you decide to publish it. Then other researchers replicate your study with other people and they find that the same relationship holds in the third-grade classrooms they studied. According to replication logic, the more times a theory or a research finding is replicated with other people, the greater the support for the theory or research finding. Now assume further that other researchers find that the relationship holds in classrooms at several other grade levels (e.g., first grade, second grade, fourth grade, and fifth grade). If this happens, the evidence suggests that the finding generalizes to students in other grade levels, adding additional generality to the finding.

We want to make one more comment before concluding. If generalizing through replication and theoretical validity (discussed above) sound similar, that is because they are. Basically, generalizing (i.e., external validity) is frequently part of theoretical validity. In other words, when researchers develop theoretical explanations, they often want to generalize beyond their

original research study. Likewise, internal validity is also important for theoretical validity if cause and effect statements are made.

## References

Brewer, J., & Hunter, A. (1989). *Multimethod research: A synthesis of styles.* Newbury Park, CA: Sage.

Campbell, D.T. (1979). Degrees of freedom and the case study. In T.D. Cook & C.S. Reichardt (Eds.), *Qualitative and quantitative methods in evaluation research* (pp. 49–67). Beverly Hills, CA: Sage Publications.

Campbell, D.T. (1986). Relabeling internal and external validity for applied social scientists. In W. Trochim (Ed.), Advances in quasi-experimental design and analysis: *New Directions for Program Evaluation*, 31, San Francisco: Jossey-Bass.

Cook, T.D., & Campbell, D.T. (1979). *Quasi-experimentation: Design and analysis issues for field settings.* Chicago: Rand McNally.

Denzin, N.K. (1989). *The research act: Theoretical introduction to sociological methods.* Englewood Cliffs, NJ: Prentice Hall.

Fetterman, D.M. (1998). Ethnography. In *Handbook of Applied Social Research Methods* by L. Bickman & D.J. Rog (Eds.). Thousand Oaks, CA: Sage.

Glaser, B.G., & Strauss, A.L. (1967). *The discovery of grounded theory: Strategies for qualitative research.* New York: Aldine de Gruyter.

Kirk, J., & Miller, M.L. (1986). *Reliability and validity in qualitative research.* Newbury Park, CA: Sage.

Johnson, R.B. (1994). Qualitative research in education. *SRATE Journal, 4*(1), 3–7.

LeCompte, M.D., & Preissle, J. (1993). *Ethnography and qualitative design in educational research.* San Diego, CA: Academic Press.

Lincoln, Y.S., & Guba, E.G. (1985). *Naturalistic inquiry.* Beverly Hills, CA: Sage.

Maxwell, J.A. (1992). Understanding and validity in qualitative research. *Harvard Educational Review, 62*(3), 279–299.

Maxwell, J.A. (1996). *Qualitative research design.* Newbury Park, CA: Sage.

Okey, T.N., & Cusick, P.A. (1995). Dropping out: Another side of the story. *Educational Administration Quarterly, 31*(2), 244–267.

Smith, J.K. (1984). The problem of criteria for judging interpretive inquiry. *Educational Evaluation and Policy Analysis, 6,* 379–391.

Smith, J.K. (1986). Closing down the conversation: The end of the quantitative-qualitative debate among educational inquirers. *Educational Researcher, 15,* 12–32.

Stake, R.E. (1990). Situational context as influence on evaluation design and use. *Studies in Educational Evaluation, 16,* 231–246.

Strauss, A. (1995). Notes on the nature and development of general theories. *Qualitative Inquiry 1*(1), 7–18.

Strauss, A., & Corbin, J. (1990). *Basics of qualitative research: Grounded theory procedures and techniques.* Newbury Park, CA: Sage.

Yin, R.K. (1994). *Case study research: Design and methods.* Newbury Park: Sage.

---

[2] The late Donald Campbell, perhaps the most important quantitative research methodologist over the past 50 years, approved of Yin's (1994) book. See, for example, his introduction to that book.

# Appendix B
# Excerpts from Two Literature Reviews

*Editor's note:* The following excerpts are presented to illustrate some principles for preparing literature reviews. First, note that each review is organized around topics (not around authors). When two or more authors report a similar finding, they are cited together. Also, note that direct quotations are used very sparingly. The sparing use of quotations increases their impact; thus, they should be used only for major points.

## *Risk Factors for Violent Juvenile Behavior*[1]

...a significant body of evidence that supports several multifaceted strategies for preventing violent crime through youth has grown. These interventions have been built upon the decades of research that has uncovered a number of robust and reliable correlates of juvenile violent behavior and overall delinquency (for a review, see Dahlberg, 1998; Hawkins, Herrenkohl et al., 1998.) From this literature, key risk factors for violent juvenile behavior have been identified that include the following: (a) family variables (e.g., poor parental supervision or parental neglect, family disruption, poor communication, parental violence); (b) individual variables (e.g., early aggressive behavior and social and cognitive processing skills deficits, such as hostile attributional bias, hyperactivity in children, and neurological impairment); (c) social variables (e.g., sibling or peer delinquency, gang membership); and (d) environmental variables (e.g., impoverished neighborhood; Elliot, 1994; Farrington, 1989; Maguin et al., 1995; Tolan & Thomas, 1995). Research has also identified critical protective factors in the prevention of youth violence (Farrington, 1993; McDonald & Sayger, 1998; Williams, 1994). Parent- and child-related factors include healthy parental attachment, high parental supervision, and high caregiver attention. In addition, family harmony, father involvement, and school bondedness have also been found to be key protective factors (Farrington, 1989; Williams, 1994).

## *Validity of Students' Evaluations of Teaching*[2]

Major reviews of the voluminous student evaluation of teaching (SET) literature (Abrami, d'Apollonia, & Cohen, 1990; Cashin, 1988; Cohen, 1987; Feldman, 1989a, 1989b, 1997, 1998; Marsh, 1984, 1987; Marsh & Dunkin, 1992; Marsh & Roche, 1994, 1997; McKeachie, 1979) have consistently shown that, with careful attention to measurement and theoretical issues, SETs are multidimensional, reliable, relatively valid in relation to various indicators of teaching effectiveness, useful for teaching improvement, and relatively unaffected by suspected biasing factors such as class size, grading leniency, and workload. Marsh (1987) concluded that SETs are probably "the most thoroughly studied of all forms of personnel evaluation, and one of the best in terms of being supported by empirical research" (p. 369). Despite such impressive support and intensive ongoing research and international growth in the successful use of SETs as one indicator of teaching quality (Marsh, 1986a; Watkins, 1994), unsubstantiated claims of potential biases in SETs continue to flourish. One particularly pervasive allegation is that to obtain good SETs, teachers need only to reduce the workload for students and give undeserved high grades (Greenwald & Gilmore, 1997a, 1997b). An implicit or explicit hypothesis in this assertion is that low workloads and easy grading standards positively bias SETs.

---

[1]From: Evans, G. D. (2001). In the echoes of gunfire: Practicing psychologists' responses to school violence. *Professional Psychology: Research and Practice, 32*, 157–164.

[2]From: Marsh, H. W., & Roche, L. A. (2000). Effects of grading leniency and low workload on students' evaluations of teaching: Popular myth, bias, validity, or innocent bystanders? *Journal of Educational Psychology, 92*, 202–228.

# Appendix C
# Indices to Journal Articles

Topic 15 illustrates some techniques for searching three electronic databases: *Sociofile*, which contains the print versions of *Sociological Abstracts* and *Social Planning/Policy & Development Abstracts*, *PsycLIT*, which contains the print version of *Psychological Abstracts*, and *ERIC*, which contains the print versions of the *Current Index to Journals in Education* (*CIJE*) and *Resources in Education* (*RIE*). The following are additional important indices and other reference tools.

## Other Electronic Indices and Abstracts

*MEDLINE* abstracts (that is, briefly summarizes) articles in more than 3,400 international journals in medicine, including psychology and psychiatry.

*Expanded Academic Index* abstracts articles in more than 1,400 scholarly and general interest journals in a variety of academic subject areas.

*Social Sciences Index* is an index to articles in more than 350 periodicals in the social sciences. It does *not* contain abstracts.

*ABI/Inform* indexes articles from over 800 business journals. For those in the social and behavioral sciences, it is strong in personnel issues, consumer behavior, organizational behavior, and human resource management.

*GENMED* is a collection of full-text databases covering the entire textual contents of major medical journals including the *Archives of General Psychiatry*, the *Journal of the American Medical Association*, and *The New England Journal of Medicine*.

## Printed Indices and Abstracts

*Social Sciences Citation Index* consists of several components, the most important of which is the *Citation Index*, which lists cited authors and their works, together with all authors who have discussed the cited works in articles. This can be very helpful in a search if you start with a classic older article that is highly relevant to your topic; by searching for all those who subsequently cited it, you can quickly build a collection of references that are likely to be very specific to your topic. Examining these sequentially permits you to trace the history of thought on a topic or theory. Other components are the *Source Index*, which provides complete bibliographic information for each article, and a *Corporate Index*.

*Dissertation Abstracts International* contains abstracts of doctoral dissertations, complete copies of which can be obtained through the publisher for a fee. *Sociofile*, an electronic database described in Topic 15, includes citations from this source since 1986 for sociology and related fields.

*Education Index* indexes articles in education but does not include abstracts. Useful for locating articles published prior to 1966, when *ERIC* (see Topic 15) was established.

OTHER MORE SPECIALIZED INDICES AND ABSTRACTS INCLUDE: *Chicano Index, Child Development Abstracts and Bibliography, Educational Administration Abstracts, Criminal Justice Periodical Index, Hispanic American Periodicals Index* (*HAPI*), *Index to Black Periodicals, Index to Legal Periodicals*, and *Women's Studies Abstracts*.

# APPENDIX D
# SELECTED SOURCES OF STATISTICAL INFORMATION

**GENERAL SOURCES:**

***Statistical Abstract of the United States.*** Washington, D.C.: U.S. Government Printing Office, 1878 to present. The premier source for finding statistics about people in the United States. Also includes international statistics that allow comparisons with U.S. data. Because the sources of the information are given, you can refer to them for additional information.

***Vital Statistics of the United States.*** Hyattsville, MD: U.S. Department of Health, Education, and Welfare, Public Health Service, National Center for Health Statistics, 1937 to present. The major source of statistics about illnesses, births, marriages, etc.

***Demographic Yearbook.*** New York: Department of Economic and Social Affairs, United Nations, 1948 to present. Statistics on health and population issues for more than 200 countries.

***World Almanac and Book of Facts.*** New York: Newspaper Enterprises Association, 1868 to present. Good source of general statistics.

**SPECIALIZED SOURCES:**

***Social Work Almanac.*** Washington, D.C.: NASW Press, 1992.

***Statistical Handbook on Aging Americans.*** Phoenix: Oryx Press, 1994.

***Statistical Handbook of the American Family.*** Phoenix: Oryx Press, 1992.

***Statistical Record of Children.*** Detroit: Gale Research, 1994.

***Statistical Handbook on Women in America.*** Phoenix: Oryx Press, 1991.

***The State of Black America.*** New York: National Urban League, 1976 to present.

***Statistical Handbook on U.S. Hispanics.*** Phoenix: Oryx Press, 1991.

***Statistical Record of Asian Americans.*** Detroit: Gale Research, 1993.

***Accident Facts.*** Itasca, IL: National Safety Council, 1927 to present.

# Appendix E
# Other Methods of Determining Reliability

In addition to interobserver, test-retest, and parallel-forms reliability (see Topic 28), we may also examine the *split-half reliability* of a test. To do this, we can treat a test given just once to a group of subjects as two tests by scoring the even-numbered items separately from the odd-numbered items. This yields two scores per subject. Calculating a correlation coefficient for them yields what is called a *split-half reliability coefficient*. Like other reliability coefficients, it ranges from 0.00 to 1.00. There are two problems with it, however. First, it is an estimate of the reliability of a test only *half as long* as the whole test. (You may recall from Topic 27 that the longer the test the higher the reliability.) A statistical adjustment, known as the Spearman-Brown Prophecy Formula, may be used to estimate the reliability of the *whole test* based on the split-half reliability of the half test.

The second problem is that the interpretation of split-half reliability coefficients is complicated by the fact that its values are dependent on the extent to which the odd-numbered items measure the same traits as the even-numbered items. Thus, the result is referred to by some as *internal consistency reliability* and by others as merely *internal consistency* (without the term *reliability*).

Somewhat analogous results can be obtained by using either *coefficient alpha* or *Kuder-Richardson Formula 20* or *21*, all of which indicate the extent to which all of the items on a test measure the same trait. Once again, these are *internal consistency* measures that also range from 0.00 to 1.00.

Information from these procedures, all of which require only one administration of a test, is of value if we want to know whether the content of a test is homogeneous (as indicated by a high coefficient). However, if we want to judge reliability as it is classically defined, the methods described in Topic 28 are preferable.

For detailed information on the assumptions underlying the various methods of examining reliability, see Thorndike, R. M. (1996). *Measurement and Evaluation in Psychology and Education.* New York: Prentice-Hall.

# APPENDIX F
# A CLOSER LOOK AT THE STANDARD DEVIATION

In this appendix, we will consider some rules for interpreting the standard deviation in relation to the normal curve as well as how to compute the standard deviation.

You learned in Topic 45 that if you go out one standard deviation unit on both sides of the mean, you capture 68% of the cases in a normal distribution. It turns out that if you go out two units on both sides of the mean, you capture approximately 95% of the cases.[1] For the distribution we considered with $M = 70$ and $S = 10$, we noted that 68% lies between scores of 60 and 80. If we go out 2 x 10 = 20 points (which is two standard deviation units) we come to scores of 50 and 90 (that is, the mean of 70 *minus* 20 = 50, and the mean of 70 *plus* 20 = 90). This is illustrated in Figure 1.

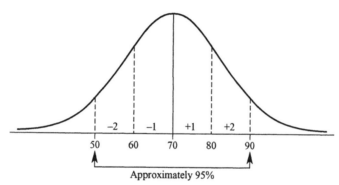

Figure 1  *Normal curve illustrating approximate 95% rule.*

If we go out three standard deviation units, we capture 99.7% of the cases, which is essentially all of them. Thus, there are about three standard deviation units on both sides of the mean in a normal distribution.

Considering how the standard deviation is calculated should give you a feeling for the meaning of the standard deviation. As the formula below indicates, it is the *square root of the mean squared deviation from the mean*. Thus, the larger the deviations from the mean, the larger the standard deviation. Conversely, the smaller the deviations from the mean, the smaller the standard deviation.

The formula that defines the standard deviation is:

$$S = \sqrt{\frac{\Sigma x^2}{N}}$$

The lower-case $x$ stands for the deviation of a score from the mean of its distribution. To obtain it, first calculate the mean (in this case, 78/6 = 13.00) and subtract the mean from each score, as shown in Example 1. Then square the deviations and sum the squares, as indicated by the symbol $\Sigma$. Then enter this value in the formula along with the number of cases ($N$) and perform the calculations as indicated in Example 1 on the next page.

---

[1]To capture precisely 95%, go out 1.96 (which is a little less than 2.00) standard deviations. If we go out 2.58 standard deviations, we capture 99% of the cases.

*Example 1:*

| Scores (X) | Deviations (X - M) | Deviations Squared ($x^2$) |
|---|---|---|
| 10 | 10 - 13.00 = -3 | 9.00 |
| 11 | 11 - 13.00 = -2 | 4.00 |
| 11 | 11 - 13.00 = -2 | 4.00 |
| 13 | 13 - 13.00 =  0 | 0.00 |
| 14 | 14 - 13.00 =  1 | 1.00 |
| 19 | 19 - 13.00 =  6 | 36.00 |
| | | $\sum x^2 = 54.00$ |

Thus, for these data:

$$S = \sqrt{\tfrac{54}{6}} = \sqrt{9.00} = 3.00$$

# APPENDIX G
# INTRODUCTION TO META-ANALYSIS

In Topic 52, you learned that an *effect size* (*d*) is a standardized measurement of the outcome of a study. For a study with two means, the effect size is calculated by dividing the difference between the two means by the standard deviation (typically, either the standard deviation of the control group or the pooled standard deviation of both groups). This statistic (*d*) standardizes the outcomes of studies since it tells us the number of standard deviation units that one group exceeds the other—regardless of the type of measure used or the number of possible score points. In other words, standardization takes place because the results of all studies in which *d* is calculated are expressed on this same standard deviation scale.

In Topic 52, you also saw how the results of a single experiment can be evaluated, with an effect size of .30 or more indicating that the study had a reasonable degree of impact, that is, when one group is about one-third of a standard deviation above the other on the average, we consider the result to be important.

A *meta-analysis* is conducted when we want to combine studies to get an overall, average effect size for a group of studies on the same general research question. For instructional purposes, let us assume that there have been only two experiments on the treatment of depression—the two in Topic 52. Since Experimenter A had an effect size of 2.5 and Experimenter B had an effect size of 0.67, we can average these to get 1.6 (2.5 + 0.67 divided by 2 = 1.6), which is an overall estimate of the effectiveness of programs for treating depression. This hypothetical result is quite large.

In a real example, researchers located 29 studies that reported on the effectiveness of supplementary one-on-one reading instruction for elementary school students judged to be at risk for reading failure. Combined, these studies contained a total of 1,539 students. (An advantage of meta-analyses is that they are often based on large numbers of participants.) By calculating the effect sizes for each of the 29 studies and averaging them, the researchers found an overall (average) value of *d* of 0.41, which is substantial.[1]

In another study, researchers found that *d* equaled 0.31 overall for a collection of studies on treatments designed to reduce HIV risks. However, when they examined specific types of risk reduction behaviors (across the collection of studies), they found considerable variation in effect sizes. For example, they obtained a value of 0.62 for risk-reduction skills but only a minuscule 0.04 for safe injection practices.[2]

Here are three important issues in the development of a meta-analytic study:

1. Could it be that all studies that are being combined in a meta-analysis contain the same bias (and, thus, all lean in the wrong direction)? For example, did all the studies use volunteers?

2. What selection standards should be used in the identification of studies to be included in a meta-analysis? Should studies that are clearly weak be omitted? If weak ones are omitted, will enough remain for a reliable meta-analysis?

3. How much caution should be given to the possibility of *publication bias* (i.e., a bias in which journals are more likely to publish studies with positive results)? Studies that are not published cannot be located for inclusion in a meta-analysis.

4. Should all studies be given equal weight in the calculation of an effect size? Generally, the answer is "no." Studies with larger numbers of participants usually should be given more weight than those with smaller sample sizes. The resulting value of *d* is referred to as a "weighted effect size."

---

[1] Source: Elbaum, B., Vaughn, S., Hughes, M. T., & Moody, S. W. (2000). How effective are one-on-one tutoring programs for elementary students at risk for reading failure? A meta-analysis of the intervention research. *Journal of Educational Psychology*, *92*, 605–619.
[2] Source: Prendergast, M. L., Urada, D., & Podus, D. (2001). Meta-analysis of HIV risk-reduction interventions within drug abuse treatment programs. *Journal of Consulting and Clinical Psychology, 69*, 389–405.

# Table 1
## Table of Random Numbers

| Row # | | | | | | | | | | | | | | | | | | |
|---|---|---|---|---|---|---|---|---|---|---|---|---|---|---|---|---|---|---|
| 1 | 2 | 1 | 0 | 4 | 9 | 8 | 0 | 8 | 8 | 8 | 0 | 6 | 9 | 2 | 4 | 8 | 2 | 6 |
| 2 | 0 | 7 | 3 | 0 | 2 | 9 | 4 | 8 | 2 | 7 | 8 | 9 | 8 | 9 | 2 | 9 | 7 | 1 |
| 3 | 4 | 4 | 9 | 0 | 0 | 2 | 8 | 6 | 2 | 6 | 7 | 7 | 7 | 3 | 1 | 2 | 5 | 1 |
| 4 | 7 | 3 | 2 | 1 | 1 | 2 | 0 | 7 | 7 | 6 | 0 | 3 | 8 | 3 | 4 | 7 | 8 | 1 |
| 5 | 3 | 3 | 2 | 5 | 8 | 3 | 1 | 7 | 0 | 1 | 4 | 0 | 7 | 8 | 9 | 3 | 7 | 7 |
| 6 | 6 | 1 | 2 | 0 | 5 | 7 | 2 | 4 | 4 | 0 | 0 | 6 | 3 | 0 | 2 | 8 | 0 | 7 |
| 7 | 7 | 0 | 9 | 3 | 3 | 3 | 7 | 4 | 0 | 4 | 8 | 8 | 9 | 3 | 5 | 8 | 0 | 5 |
| 8 | 7 | 5 | 1 | 9 | 0 | 9 | 1 | 5 | 2 | 6 | 5 | 0 | 9 | 0 | 3 | 5 | 8 | 8 |
| 9 | 3 | 5 | 6 | 9 | 6 | 5 | 0 | 1 | 9 | 4 | 6 | 6 | 7 | 5 | 6 | 8 | 3 | 1 |
| 10 | 8 | 5 | 0 | 3 | 9 | 4 | 3 | 4 | 0 | 6 | 5 | 1 | 7 | 4 | 4 | 6 | 2 | 7 |
| 11 | 0 | 5 | 9 | 6 | 8 | 7 | 4 | 8 | 1 | 5 | 5 | 0 | 5 | 1 | 7 | 1 | 5 | 8 |
| 12 | 7 | 6 | 2 | 2 | 6 | 9 | 6 | 1 | 9 | 7 | 1 | 1 | 4 | 7 | 1 | 6 | 2 | 0 |
| 13 | 3 | 8 | 4 | 7 | 8 | 9 | 8 | 2 | 2 | 1 | 6 | 3 | 8 | 7 | 0 | 4 | 6 | 1 |
| 14 | 1 | 9 | 1 | 8 | 4 | 5 | 6 | 1 | 8 | 1 | 2 | 4 | 4 | 4 | 2 | 7 | 3 | 4 |
| 15 | 1 | 5 | 3 | 6 | 7 | 6 | 1 | 8 | 4 | 3 | 1 | 8 | 8 | 7 | 7 | 6 | 0 | 4 |
| 16 | 0 | 5 | 5 | 3 | 6 | 0 | 7 | 1 | 3 | 8 | 1 | 4 | 6 | 7 | 0 | 4 | 3 | 5 |
| 17 | 2 | 2 | 3 | 8 | 6 | 0 | 9 | 1 | 9 | 0 | 4 | 4 | 7 | 6 | 8 | 1 | 5 | 1 |
| 18 | 2 | 3 | 3 | 2 | 5 | 5 | 7 | 6 | 9 | 4 | 9 | 7 | 1 | 3 | 7 | 9 | 3 | 8 |
| 19 | 8 | 5 | 5 | 0 | 5 | 3 | 7 | 8 | 5 | 4 | 5 | 1 | 6 | 0 | 4 | 8 | 9 | 1 |
| 20 | 0 | 6 | 1 | 1 | 3 | 4 | 8 | 6 | 4 | 3 | 2 | 9 | 4 | 3 | 8 | 7 | 4 | 1 |
| 21 | 9 | 1 | 1 | 8 | 2 | 9 | 0 | 6 | 9 | 6 | 9 | 4 | 2 | 9 | 9 | 0 | 6 | 0 |
| 22 | 3 | 7 | 8 | 0 | 6 | 3 | 7 | 1 | 2 | 6 | 5 | 2 | 7 | 6 | 5 | 6 | 5 | 1 |
| 23 | 5 | 3 | 0 | 5 | 1 | 2 | 1 | 0 | 9 | 1 | 3 | 7 | 5 | 6 | 1 | 2 | 5 | 0 |
| 24 | 7 | 2 | 4 | 8 | 6 | 7 | 9 | 3 | 8 | 7 | 6 | 0 | 9 | 1 | 6 | 5 | 7 | 8 |
| 25 | 0 | 9 | 1 | 6 | 7 | 0 | 3 | 8 | 0 | 9 | 1 | 5 | 4 | 2 | 3 | 2 | 4 | 5 |
| 26 | 3 | 8 | 1 | 4 | 3 | 7 | 9 | 2 | 4 | 5 | 1 | 2 | 8 | 7 | 7 | 4 | 1 | 3 |

# Table 2
## Table of Recommended Sample Sizes (*n*) for Populations (*N*) with Finite Sizes[1]

| *N* | *n* | *N* | *n* | *N* | *n* |
|---|---|---|---|---|---|
| 10 | 10 | 220 | 140 | 1,200 | 291 |
| 15 | 14 | 230 | 144 | 1,300 | 297 |
| 20 | 19 | 240 | 148 | 1,400 | 302 |
| 25 | 24 | 250 | 152 | 1,500 | 306 |
| 30 | 28 | 260 | 155 | 1,600 | 310 |
| 35 | 32 | 270 | 159 | 1,700 | 313 |
| 40 | 36 | 280 | 162 | 1,800 | 317 |
| 45 | 40 | 290 | 165 | 1,900 | 320 |
| 50 | 44 | 300 | 169 | 2,000 | 322 |
| 55 | 48 | 320 | 175 | 2,200 | 327 |
| 60 | 52 | 340 | 181 | 2,400 | 331 |
| 65 | 56 | 360 | 186 | 2,600 | 335 |
| 70 | 59 | 380 | 191 | 2,800 | 338 |
| 75 | 63 | 400 | 196 | 3,000 | 341 |
| 80 | 66 | 420 | 201 | 3,500 | 346 |
| 85 | 70 | 440 | 205 | 4,000 | 351 |
| 90 | 73 | 460 | 210 | 4,500 | 354 |
| 95 | 76 | 480 | 214 | 5,000 | 357 |
| 100 | 80 | 500 | 217 | 6,000 | 361 |
| 110 | 86 | 550 | 226 | 7,000 | 364 |
| 120 | 92 | 600 | 234 | 8,000 | 367 |
| 130 | 97 | 650 | 242 | 9,000 | 368 |
| 140 | 103 | 700 | 248 | 10,000 | 370 |
| 150 | 108 | 750 | 254 | 15,000 | 375 |
| 160 | 113 | 800 | 260 | 20,000 | 377 |
| 170 | 118 | 850 | 265 | 30,000 | 379 |
| 180 | 123 | 900 | 269 | 40,000 | 380 |
| 190 | 127 | 950 | 274 | 50,000 | 381 |
| 200 | 132 | 1,000 | 278 | 75,000 | 382 |
| 210 | 136 | 1,100 | 285 | 100,000 | 384 |

[1]Adapted from: Krejcie, R. V. & Morgan, D. W. (1970). Determining sample size for researc' *Educational and Psychological Measurement, 30,* 607–610.

# Index